Words matter—they matter a lot—a them wisely and well. This book off the everyday kinds of interactions we chapter provides fuel for reflection, hope. Rooted in Scripture and grounded in real life, this is an accessible, engaging resource, packed full of wisdom.

HELEN THORNE, Director of Training and Resources, Biblical Counselling UK

In this inspiring book, Carolyn Lacey helps us to appreciate just how important words are—helping us to see how our words can become channels of blessing into the lives of others. It is not just a matter of avoiding toxic words. Carolyn engages with a wide range of biblical passages in a way which is both pastorally sensitive and very challenging. Each chapter ends with a series of questions which enable the reader to apply what they have learned. Highly recommended.

PAUL MALLARD, Author; Speaker

As someone who regularly speaks before I think, I am accustomed to putting my foot in my mouth, as the saying goes! As I read these pages, I was both challenged and comforted. Carolyn Lacey doses out just the right amount of both truth and grace. She prioritizes the goodness we see in God's word and in God himself, and then she helps us to ponder how our own words might reflect that goodness in all kinds of situations. If you struggle with what to say or how to say it, this book will strengthen you!

JEN OSHMAN, Author, *Cultural Counterfeits*

Our God is a speaking God, and he always says the right thing at the right time and in the right way. As his people, we are to speak words that bring life and love to each other and to the world we live in. And this book wonderfully captures the essence of what that means for us in a world where words seem to do more damage than good. I finished *Say the Right Thing* being more aware of how I use my words, and realising not just that I need the help of the Lord in every conversation and interaction to speak in a way that glorifies him, but also that there is joy and blessing in being a person who says the right thing. This book shines bright in a world of words that are so often dark and destructive. A must-read for all who use words.

STEVE ROBINSON, Senior Pastor, Cornerstone Church Liverpool

Taming the tongue is a daunting task. James warns us of the damage our words can do, and we know we mustn't lie, slander or blaspheme—so how can we train our tongues (and our written words) and use them for good? In this little book, Carolyn Lacey looks at seven godly ways to use our words. With practical, honest examples, she helps us see how the things we say can bring beauty, hope, comfort and more to a world where words tear down more often than they build up. Insightful and encouraging.

JENNIE POLLOCK, Author, *If Only*

Given that the primary way we interact with other people is by speaking, it is unsurprising that the Bible has much to say about how we speak. However, speech is often a neglected aspect of our sanctification. This fresh and challenging book reminds us of the importance and beauty of godly speech. It expounds key biblical passages in a clear and compelling way, and applies them to everyday life with engaging illustrations, examples, personal testimony and searching questions for reflection at the end of each short chapter. It will help readers to guard their tongues, bless others and honour Jesus with their words.

JOHN STEVENS, National Director, FIEC

Say the Right Thing

CAROLYN LACEY

Say the Right Thing
© Carolyn Lacey, 2023.

Published by:
The Good Book Company

thegoodbook.com | thegoodbook.co.uk
thegoodbook.com.au | thegoodbook.co.nz | thegoodbook.co.in

The author photograph was taken by Megan Cobbett.

ISBN: 9781784988692 | Printed in the UK

Design by Drew McCall

*Let the words of my mouth
and the meditation of my heart
be acceptable in your sight,
O LORD, my rock and my redeemer.*

Psalm 19 v 14 (ESV)

Carolyn Lacey is a church women's
worker, pastor's wife and mother
to two grown-up children. Based
in Worcester, UK, she teaches the
Bible regularly at women's events and
conferences. She is also the author
of *Extraordinary Hospitality
(For Ordinary People)*.

CONTENTS

INTRODUCTION

I don't always say the right thing.

Like you (I imagine), I know the shame of saying the wrong thing and only realising when it is too late. And the feeling of wanting to say the right thing, but not knowing what it is. None of us use our words well all of the time.

But I have also experienced the life-giving gift of a kind word spoken at just the right moment, the soul-nourishing goodness of a loving correction offered by someone wanting to help me grow in godliness. There are simple but significant reminders that God can use our speech—imperfect as it is—to encourage, equip and sustain his people as they seek to live for him.

Solomon says that "a word spoken at the right time is like gold apples in silver settings" (Proverbs 25 v 11, CSB) and "the tongue that heals is a tree of life" (Proverbs 15 v 4, CSB). I would like my words to have this kind of positive impact in the lives of those I speak to. And if you've picked up this book, I imagine that you would too. The good news is that they can!

When I was growing up, I heard a lot about the "do nots" of godly speech: do not lie, do not swear, do not blaspheme, do not gossip, do not exaggerate, do not praise yourself, do not slander other people, do not talk back to parents or teachers. (You can probably add to the list.) This was all good advice for staying out of trouble—and many of these instructions correspond to the Bible's teaching about godly speech. But my problem was that, while I was fairly clear about what I should not say, I was left wondering what should replace these ungodly patterns of speech. What should I say, instead? Perhaps you have wondered the same thing.

The Bible offers a vision for our speech that goes beyond simply being well-mannered and not causing harm. It shows how our words can have a hugely positive impact on those around us—in a variety of ways and in different contexts. Our words have the power to bring healing to those who are hurting. To bring peace and reconciliation where there is conflict and fear. To offer hope to those living in despair. To give joy to those who are sorrowful. To combat lies with truth. To speak wisdom and beauty and grace into the lives of those around us. And to witness to God's goodness and glory whenever we have the opportunity.

My aim in this book is not to tell you what you should or shouldn't say. Instead, I want to explore this hopeful vision for our speech and to equip you to put it into practice—as well as to encourage you that this isn't something we have to try to achieve by ourselves. Only God can shape our speech so that it produces good fruit, in us and in our hearers. But the Bible's encouragement is that he is willing and able to do so.

Saying the right thing is not about being nice or polite: sometimes it means speaking the truth when people don't want to hear it, or calling out wrong thinking and behaviour. Saying the right thing is about using our words to do good to the people we encounter each day, whether that's in the home, workplace, church, local community, or on social media. It's about letting our speech be shaped by God's word rather than the world. And it's about looking to bring glory to him in every conversation or interaction. This is not something only super-saints can do. Each of us can learn to use our words—spoken or online—to make a difference to the people in our lives.

How do we cultivate wise speech? In a post-truth culture, what is the impact of speaking truth to one another? What does it really mean to be kind with our words? How can we use our words to bring beauty into view? These are some of the questions we will explore over the next seven chapters. As we do, I pray that you will be encouraged to consider the amazing things God can accomplish through your words, and be more equipped to glorify him with your speech.

By his power [may God] fulfil your every desire to do good, so that the name of our Lord Jesus will be glorified. (2 Thessalonians 1 v 11-12)

HOW TO AVOID THAT
SINKING FEELING

SPEAKING WISDOM

*My dear brothers and sisters, take note of this:
everyone should be quick to listen, slow to
speak and slow to become angry.*

James 1 v 19

On 31st October 1938, actor and screenwriter Orson Welles found himself at the centre of a media storm. The previous evening, Welles and his theatre company had performed an adaptation of H.G. Wells' novel, *The War of the Worlds*, on his radio show. Welles had creatively converted the novel into a series of fake news bulletins describing a Martian invasion of New Jersey. But while a fictional news reporter choked on poison gas and imaginary Martians overpowered New York, confused listeners mistook the play's bulletins for live news reports, and widespread panic followed.

While few people really believed Martians were attacking, many were convinced they were listening to reports of a German invasion, and their frightened phone calls to radio stations and newspaper offices convinced journalists that Orson Welles' show had caused nationwide hysteria. Welles woke the next morning to reports of chaos across the country and angry listeners threatening to shoot him for causing such distress. What started out as a bit of creative fun turned into a nightmare for Welles. "If I'd planned to wreck my career," he said, "I couldn't have gone about it better".

Welles had no idea beforehand what effect his words would have—and once he did, it was too late. Just imagine the sinking feeling as he became aware of the consequences of his mistake. His sense of guilt as he understood the hurt he had caused. The knot in the pit of his stomach as he anticipated the damage to his career prospects.

They're familiar feelings, aren't they? While you or I may not have the influence to cause nationwide hysteria with our words, we all know what it's like to feel embarrassment, shame or regret over speaking before thinking. How many times have you wished you had stayed silent in a meeting instead of saying something foolish or unhelpful? How many nights have you spent lying awake replaying an insensitive or hurtful response to a friend or family member's problems? It's easy to rush in with thoughtless or inappropriate words. It's much harder to undo the damage our hasty words may cause—to us as well as to our hearers.

It doesn't have to be this way, though. The apostle James writes:

> *The wisdom that comes from heaven is first of all pure; then peace-loving, considerate, submissive, full of mercy and good fruit, impartial and sincere. Peacemakers who sow in peace reap a harvest of righteousness. (James 3 v 17-18)*

It is possible to learn to speak with wisdom from heaven that will impact our everyday conversations on Earth—so that we speak wise words, in a wise way, that will reap a harvest of righteousness in the people around us. This is what we are going to focus on in this chapter. But if that feels a little out of reach, don't worry—James helps us understand why.

LITTLE FIRES EVERYWHERE

Earlier in his letter, James paints a powerful portrait of the tongue. He compares it to a raging fire that consumes and corrupts; a reckless killer running wild and unrestrained. It may be small, but no other part of the body has such power.

> *The tongue is a small part of the body, but it makes great boasts. Consider what a great forest is set on fire by a small spark. The tongue also is a fire, a world of evil among the parts of the body. It corrupts the whole body, sets the whole course of one's life on fire, and is itself set on fire by hell … It is a restless evil, full of deadly poison. (James 3 v 5-6, 8)*

I wonder how often you think about the power of your tongue in this way. I rarely do! But every day, you and I enter homes, colleges, workplaces, shops, hospitals, banks and churches carrying a weapon poised for mass destruction. And we rarely stop to think about the chaos we could inflict with it. An irritable tone can send a child running to their bedroom in tears. A harsh comment can hurt or embitter a loved one for years to come. "Harmless" banter can humiliate or deflate a brother or sister in Christ. A piece of gossip can shred a reputation or fracture a friendship.

You can probably think of ways in which you have been hurt by someone else's words, even if it was only fleetingly. Perhaps you've felt undermined by a work colleague's response to ideas you've shared in a meeting. Maybe discouraging remarks made by a teacher still linger in your memory. Perhaps you replay the constant criticism you received from a parent—or contrast it with the approval they showed to a favoured sibling. Maybe you feel you're always the target of your friends' jokes.

I have a friend who struggled for a decade with an eating disorder which she traces back to a grandparent's constant criticism of her figure during her teens. I recently read about a doctor whose reputation was ruined by an unhappy patient who spread false rumours about his unprofessional conduct. And we all know of family relationships that have been torn apart by unkind words spoken in anger.

We do not need to look far to find evidence of the tongue's destructive power. That's why if we want to learn to speak wisely, there's an unexpected first step: before we think about what to say, we need to consider whether to say anything at all. Wise speech is slow and thoughtful.

We must take note of James' warning to be "quick to listen, slow to speak" (James 1 v 19).

During the Second World War, the US Office of War Information coined the phrase, "Loose lips might sink ships". (It's easy to remember but hard to say quickly!) The phrase was part of a campaign to limit the possibility of people unintentionally giving useful information to enemy spies. Various other slogans emerged around the world, all under the campaign's basic message: "Careless talk costs lives". We'd do well to apply that kind of message to our own use of words.

THE WISDOM OF GOD

So what's the solution? Is it actually possible to do good and not harm with our words, or are we fighting a losing battle with our tongues? Maybe silence really is golden, and the best thing is to say nothing at all!

Except I'm sure you can think of people who do always seem to know the right thing to say. Their speech is full of wisdom, insight and peace—just as James describes. My friend Jamie is like that. She is calm and measured in her speech. She doesn't interrupt, and she doesn't trivialise serious problems with quick solutions. I'm always struck by her gentleness and grace. What's her secret?

Firstly, she listens. She doesn't offer advice until she's really understood the problem. She doesn't pass a judgment on the situation until she's sure of the facts. This takes time! In our hit-send-think-later culture it doesn't come naturally for us to stop speaking and assess a situation with a clear head—and then to pray for wisdom before we respond. But taking time to listen well increases the likelihood of answering well.

Secondly, Jamie speaks with wisdom because she is learning from Jesus, the wisdom of God (1 Corinthians 1 v 24). Perhaps you sometimes think, *If only Jesus lived on earth today. Then he could just tell me what the right words or actions are.* But Jesus speaks to us by his Spirit every time we open his word. He doesn't answer every question about every dilemma we face. But as we read his word, he helps us grow in wisdom so we can respond in the way he would want.

Perhaps this is most obvious when speaking wisely isn't so much about what we say as how we say it. A few years ago, I spent some weeks memorising and meditating on Paul's letter to the Ephesians. Not long after, I found myself in a frustrating situation with someone who was being particularly unkind in the way they spoke to me. My natural impulse was to bite back with a harsh rebuke, but before I could, words that had become familiar came to mind:

> *Be completely humble and gentle; be patient, bearing with one another in love. (Ephesians 4 v 2)*

The Spirit brought to mind the truth I needed to help me respond wisely, and the tension was quickly diffused. Time spent in God's word was renewing my mind and transforming my heart—and that impacted my speech.

This shouldn't surprise us. Israel's wisest king, Solomon, writes in Proverbs 9 v 10:

The fear of the LORD is the beginning of wisdom.

So if we want to grow in wisdom—both in the tone and in the content of what we say—we need to know God more through his word. We need to immerse ourselves in the word and submit to the Spirit's transforming work in us as we humbly obey it.

WISE HEARTS, WISE SPEECH

The reason we need to focus on knowing and being transformed by God is that speaking wisely isn't simply about managing our tongues moment-by-moment, nor just about giving prudent and insightful advice. It goes deeper than that—to our hearts. After his vivid description of the tongue, James lays down a challenge: if you think you're wise, show it by your life (James 3 v 13). It's not such an abrupt change of topic as we may think. In the previous verses, James has shown that our words simply reflect what's in our hearts. Just as the fruit that falls from a tree shows what type of tree it is, so the words that fall from our lips show what kind of heart we have (v 12). He is echoing Jesus' teaching in Matthew 12:

> *For the mouth speaks what the heart is full of. A good man brings good things out of the good stored up in him, and an evil man brings evil things out of the evil stored up in him. (Matthew 12 v 34-35)*

Rash, foolish and damaging speech is the fruit of a heart that is proud, full of bitter envy and selfish ambition (James 3 v 14). But the wisdom that God gives results in pure hearts and fruitful speech. Wise speech can't be separated from wise hearts. Rather, it's through our speech that it becomes clear whether or not our hearts are wise.

We sometimes think that wisdom just means good advice—a wise person is someone with enough life experience to advise the right course of action. But look again at James 3 v 17-18:

> *But the wisdom that comes from heaven is first of all pure; then peace-loving, considerate, submissive, full of mercy and good fruit, impartial and sincere. Peacemakers who sow in peace reap a harvest of righteousness.*

This is the kind of speech that will be native to us as we grow in wisdom. It's the opposite of an out-of-control tongue, and it's much better than just giving sensible advice! My words can be pure. My speech can be peaceable, considerate, humble, merciful, fair and sincere. It can reflect the good fruit Jesus is growing in me as I abide in him. And it can result not just in someone making a prudent decision but in something much greater: a harvest of righteousness. Isn't that a hopeful picture?

Speaking in this way will mean, firstly, that our speech will honour God. We will want to talk about him more than we talk about ourselves. We will want to draw attention to the things that are beautiful, good and true. We will be quick to offer words of thanks and appreciation, forgiveness and reconciliation. We will use our words to speak on behalf of those who suffer injustice.

We will let our conversations be "always full of grace" (Colossians 4 v 6).

But secondly, it means that others will be drawn closer to him through our words. If we use our words wisely, we can expect others to be impacted for good. As we hold back from speaking rash and angry words and instead choose gentleness, we may diffuse a quarrel before it gets going. We may keep ourselves from sin—and the person we're speaking to as well. As we choose merciful words over impatient or critical speech, we build up the person we are speaking to rather than tearing them down. As we respond fairly and without favouritism to a quarrel between family members or neighbours, we communicate respect and honour to them.

Solomon writes:

> *The words of the reckless pierce like swords, but the tongue of the wise brings healing. (Proverbs 12 v 18)*

We don't have to look too hard to see the first half of this proverb illustrated—especially on social media. It's never been easier to join in with criticism and caricaturing of individuals we have never met and know little about. And although we might not give much thought to our tweets or posts, they can contribute to the ruin of reputations, relationships and lives. We may as well be brandishing swords.

But it doesn't have to be like this. While the reckless cause pain and suffering with their uncontrolled tongues (and thumbs!), the wise can bring refreshment and healing. We can choose to believe the best and forgive the worst.

To love our friend or family member more than we love winning an argument. To treat people we find difficult with civility rather than contempt. To use our words—spoken or written—to encourage, endorse and equip. This is what it really means to speak wisdom.

Sadly, it's worth adding that not every relationship can be healed and helped by wise words. Sometimes, despite our best efforts, people continue to pursue conflict and hurt. In such situations, even our wisest words are not enough—we have to step away, whether for a time or for ever.

But this is not the case in the majority of situations. So, assuming that is not your experience, I invite you to consider: when do you most often find yourself speaking rashly or impatiently? Who do you tend to speak to aggressively rather than with consideration and gentleness? In what situations do you tend towards unfairness or bitterness in your speech? Stop for a moment now and ask God to change your heart and make it pure and peace-loving so that your words will be full of mercy and good fruit. And so that your tongue will not bring harm but healing.

HABITS OF WISDOM

While prayer is the first step in cultivating wise speech, some practical tips can also help. We've seen that the best way of becoming wise is to saturate ourselves in God's word. But what about in our moment-by-moment interactions? How can we train ourselves to say the right thing when difficult conversations take us by surprise? Or when we disagree with something a friend or co-worker says?

One key piece of advice is simply to listen—like my

friend Jamie does. Proverbs 18 v 13 tells us, "To answer before listening—that is folly and shame".

Listening is hard. It requires humility and self-control. When we interrupt people, we show that we care more about what we want to say than what they want to share. We presume our words are more necessary or interesting or helpful than others' words. When we monopolise a group chat or work meeting or Bible study with our own viewpoints, we neglect to honour others who may also have valuable contributions to make and instead elevate ourselves as the most important speaker in the room. We may not do it intentionally, but our tongues reveal our pride and lack of restraint.

So how do we learn to slow down—to be quick to listen and slow to speak? Here are a few questions we could internally ask ourselves before diving into a conversation:

- Have I listened carefully to what this person is saying? Have I fully understood or do I need to ask them to explain what they mean?
- Am I being asked my opinion/advice or just to listen and understand?
- Do I have anything helpful to contribute to the conversation? Is someone else able to bring more wisdom/experience/knowledge to the situation?
- What could I say to diffuse tension or anger?
- What could I say to encourage, comfort or support?
- Will my words help or harm?

It's not a failsafe way to guard against sin, but getting

into the habit of thinking before we speak may limit the damage we do with our words. I like the NLT paraphrase of Proverbs 10 v 19:

> *Too much talk leads to sin. Be sensible and keep your mouth shut.*

I've said that the tongue reveals what is going on in the heart, but it can work the other way too. For example, speaking unkindly about someone can encourage unkind feelings we have towards them, while choosing to say something appreciative can increase feelings of appreciation or respect. So training and taming the tongue is a way of training and taming the heart.

You may be thinking: what about when I am the one sinned against? Do we still need to be slow to speak when people are saying unkind, unfair or untrue things to us? In Frances Hodgson Burnett's book, *The Little Princess*, 11-year-old Sara Crewe proves she is far wiser than I often am. Her advice?

> *When people are insulting you, there is nothing so good for them as not to say a word—just to look at them and think. When you will not fly into a passion people know you are stronger than they are, because you are strong enough to hold in your rage, and they are not, and they say stupid things they wished they hadn't said afterward. There's nothing so strong as rage, except what makes you hold it in—that's stronger. It's a good thing not to answer your enemies.*
> *(A Little Princess, p 115)*

Of course, that's easier said than done—and some of us especially struggle to control our anger. But if multiplying words multiplies sin, keeping quiet is a sensible instinct—at least until we've had time to think and pray about our response. When someone is being unkind or unfair to me, I have found it helpful to inwardly recite, "This is a person made in God's image; treat them with dignity". If the person offending me is a Christian, I will tell myself, "This is a brother/sister for whom Christ died. Do not dishonour him by dishonouring them." It's taken a while for these responses to come naturally (and I still fail frequently), but regular practice has helped. Perhaps you could try something similar the next time someone sins against you with their words. (And, if you really can't control your tongue, there is always the option to walk away before saying something you will later regret!)

THE POWER OF LIFE

James says that the tongue is so restless and full of evil that no human being can tame it (James 3 v 8). But the good news is that, while we may not be able to tame our tongues, God can. The answer to the problem of an uncontrollable tongue is to deal with the heart it reveals. And God is able to renew our hearts (Ezekiel 36 v 26). He can transform them from being self-loving and self-focused to Christ-loving and others-focused. He can exchange our tendency towards sin into a desire for goodness. He can ignite passion for his glory and honour rather than our own. The result will be a tongue that becomes an instrument of righteousness. This will benefit us as well as those we speak to. Solomon says:

> *From the fruit of their mouth a person's stomach is filled; with the harvest of their lips they are satisfied. The tongue has the power of life and death, and those who love it will eat its fruit. (Proverbs 18 v 20-21)*

Picture a hardworking farmer diligently sowing seed and planting vegetables. She takes care over her work so that when it is time to harvest, her stomach may be filled and she may be satisfied. If the harvest is poor, she will go hungry and her family may starve to death. Her life and the lives of others depends on her work, so she pours everything into it. Every task is undertaken with love and care.

In the same way, we need to take care over our words—because they will either produce a good or poor harvest. When we choose rash, unkind, belittling, critical, untrue words, they damage our souls as well as hurting others. We regret the hurt we cause to those we care about. We feel ashamed of our lack of self-control. We fear retaliation—or that people will think less of us. Our tongues wound us as well as those around us.

But there is a better way. When we speak words that are true, hopeful, encouraging, kind and comforting, we will be satisfied with the good fruit they produce. We will experience joy as we see others grow and flourish because of our encouragement. We will be grateful for opportunities to bring comfort and healing to those who are suffering. And we will be content knowing that whatever the human response, our words have pleased our heavenly Father.

There is no quick or easy path to wisdom—and some-times, that's frustrating. But if wisdom leads to life, it's definitely a path worth choosing.

QUESTIONS FOR REFLECTION

1. *Do you ever think about your tongue as a weapon? How might remembering its power—to harm or heal—affect your day-to-day speech?*

2. *Think of someone you consider to be wise in the way they speak. What is distinctive about the way they listen and respond in conversation? What could you learn from them?*

3. *In what situations do you most often find yourself speaking before thinking? What will help you remember to pause, pray and listen well before responding?*

4. *Solomon says, "The tongue of the wise brings healing" (Proverbs 12 v 18). In what situations could your words bring healing to someone right now?*

BUILD THE BODY

SPEAKING TRUTH

*Each of you must put off falsehood and speak
truthfully to your neighbour, for we are all members
of one body.*

Ephesians 4 v 25

In March 2021, millions of people on both sides of the Atlantic tuned in to watch Oprah Winfrey's interview with the Duke and Duchess of Sussex, Harry and Meghan. A phrase from the teaser clip caught my attention. Oprah asked Meghan, "How do you feel about the palace hearing you speak your truth today?"

Speak your truth. That interview wasn't the first time Oprah had used this expression. When she accepted her Lifetime Achievement Award at the 2018 Golden Globes, she confidently declared, "What I know for sure is that speaking your truth is the most powerful tool we all have".

It sounds compelling. After all, who knows your story better than you? Who can argue against the truth as you have experienced it—*your* truth? And how can you be the most authentic version of yourself if you do not speak your truth?

But *speaking my truth* is powerful only until my truth butts heads with another person's opposing truth. When our truths collide and conflict, whose truth will win? Inevitably, the truth of the person who is more powerful, more eloquent or more influential. *Speak your truth* is an empowering philosophy only until my truth causes pain for those around me. Until it isolates me from family members or friends who find my truth hurtful and destructive. Until it leaves me lonely and without anyone to enjoy my truth with.

When Oprah asked Meghan how she felt about the palace hearing her speak her truth, the implication was that it could potentially cause a rift in her relationships with other members of the Royal Family. And she had a point! Let's say you feel exasperated by your sister's inability to make decisions as quickly as you do or to follow through on commitments as consistently as you do. While your frustrations may be justifiable, if you speak your truth at the wrong time in the wrong tone, you risk hurting her and fracturing your relationship. How about when a friend from church talks to you about a sinful pattern of behaviour he is trying to address that, in your opinion, he should have faced up to years ago? If you speak your truth too eagerly, you will likely damage your friendship and miss an opportunity to help him grow and mature in his faith.

Speak your truth may sound like a liberating philosophy but it is deeply flawed. The Bible commands each of us not to speak *your* truth, but to speak *the* truth. And the purpose of truth-speaking is not simply to share our story or vent our emotions—important though those things are sometimes. The biblical reason for speaking the truth is spiritual maturity. Not just individual maturity, but the growth and maturity of the whole body of believers.

I wonder if you have thought about that before. God's will for your words is that they should result in the body of Christ growing to maturity. How will this happen? What is the truth we should speak to one another? And how can we overcome some of the obstacles that get in the way of doing this?

BODY BUILDING

In his letter to the Ephesians, the apostle Paul writes:

> *Each of you must put off falsehood and speak truthfully to your neighbour, for we are all members of one body. (Ephesians 4 v 25)*

Included in his instruction is the motivation for speaking truthfully: we are members of one body. Paul does not say that the reason for speaking truthfully is because God hates lying (Proverbs 6 v 16-17), or because the ninth commandment instructs us not to give false testimony against our neighbour (Exodus 20 v 16). Instead, he roots this instruction in our corporate identity as Christ's body. We should speak the truth to one another because we are members of the same body, and our goal is to mature as a body. Paul reminds his readers of this just a few verses earlier:

Speaking the truth in love, we will grow to become in every respect the mature body of him who is the head, that is, Christ. (Ephesians 4 v 15)

When he says, "speaking the truth in love", Paul is confronting two common tendencies in responding to the sins and weaknesses of other believers. The first is confusing love with comfort.

Sometimes we are tempted to believe that loving someone means overlooking those parts of their life that dishonour Christ. We might avoid talking about biblical teaching that contradicts our friend's beliefs or behaviour. We prefer to enjoy comfortable but shallow relationships rather than open doors to potential awkwardness or misunderstanding. I can think of plenty of times when I've known I should confront a friend about something unkind or untrue they've said about another person, or about their tendency to criticise or complain, but I couldn't face the discomfort. I typically put off having those conversations for as long as possible.

The second is being so committed to the truth that we care more about tearing down false thinking than building up with the truth. We often use the phrase "speaking the truth in love" as a kind of Christian equivalent of *Speak your truth*. It can be used as an excuse for saying whatever we want to say to someone—as long as we say it with a loving tone! But this isn't the kind of truth-telling Paul has in view. He is not giving permission for believers to get things off their chest so they can feel better. No, his goal is that as members of Christ's body speak the truth to one another, they will grow more and more like him. And to do so "in love" does not simply mean using a loving tone. It means thinking about the purpose and potential result of our words.

Jesus has designed his body to be nurtured and nourished with his word—the word of truth (Psalm 119 v 43). So speaking the truth in love is less about correcting every viewpoint we disagree with or every under-developed belief another believer expresses, and everything to do with building one another up with the word of truth in a manner that is loving and reflective of Jesus.

This doesn't mean that we shouldn't call out behaviour that is not Christlike—that would not be loving. But our goal is not simply correction. And our motive is not primarily frustration. When we challenge ungodly behaviour, it should be out of a sincere desire for every part of the body to become more like Christ. That means we not only call someone *out* on sin, but we also call them *to* holiness. We are not calling them to behaviour that we approve of or that conforms to our own, but to behaviour that conforms to the teaching we find in God's word.

It is God's word that is *the* truth, not ours. So speaking the truth in love means speaking the truth of his word—whether we are addressing behaviour or beliefs.

Biblical scholar Greg Beale writes:

Our growth into maturity in Christ is only possible by constant and ongoing exposure to the word of God

through one another … The temple of Christ's body
and dwelling place of God grows by means of the word
of God spoken by believers to one another.
(God Dwells Among Us, p 106)

Speaking the truth of God's word to one another will cause us to grow up into Christ. That is what will stop us from being "tossed back and forth by the waves, and blown here and there by every wind of teaching" (Ephesians 4 v 14). And if our goal is to strengthen and build the body, we will do this from a disposition of love. Not with a desire to point-score, belittle or parade our own knowledge, but with an earnest desire for the body—individuals and the whole—to become more like Christ.

This means speaking with humility, gentleness and patience rather than self-importance, irritability or anger. It means being careful to point to what the Bible actually says rather than how we may have chosen to apply it. It means focusing any correction on core gospel issues rather than matters of personal preference or conscience. Choose to care about whether your friend is relying on Jesus' perfect life and death for salvation rather than her own righteousness. Be less concerned about whether she pops to the supermarket on a Sunday.

It's not easy, is it? I imagine that, depending on your personality, you will veer towards one tendency or another. You may be so committed to truth-telling that you don't stop to consider whether what you have to say is said out of love with the goal of building up. Or you may be so committed to loving well that you shy away from speaking the truth if there is a risk of awkwardness or offence.

Whatever our natural tendency may be, we need wisdom and help to become body-builders, rather than truth-obscurers. But when we are willing to put aside both our need to be right and our need for approval, the Spirit can use our words to strengthen our brothers and sisters in faith, and to help the body become more like the head.

LESSONS FROM A PROPHET

When God sent the prophet Nathan to speak the truth to King David, Nathan would have been aware of the risk. David was the most powerful man in Israel. Nathan had spoken God's word to him before, but that was when God promised blessing for David and his descendants (2 Samuel 7). There was little cost in telling the truth in that situation. But now that Nathan had to confront David about his sin, the stakes were higher. David might respond in a fit of rage and have Nathan killed—after all, he had already commanded the killing of another man who had threatened his comfort (2 Samuel 11 v 15).

For years David had sought to worship, honour and serve the Lord with all his heart, but in this season he chose self-love over devotion to the Lord. He sent the fighting men of Israel off to war, but stayed at home in luxury and comfort. He took Bathsheba—another man's wife—and got her pregnant. Then, instead of repenting and accepting the consequences, he tried to cover it up. He arranged for Bathsheba's husband, Uriah, to come back from the war and spend the night with his wife so that everyone would assume the child was Uriah's. But Uriah did not fall in line with David's plans, so David had him sent to the front line of battle where he would be killed. It was brutal and cowardly. David abused his position and power to destroy another man's life.

And he did not repent quickly. He took Bathsheba into the palace as his wife and hardened his heart against the Lord for many months. It was only when Nathan confronted him about his sin that David confessed and was restored.

Why did you despise the word of the LORD by doing what is evil in his eyes? You struck down Uriah the Hittite with the sword and took his wife to be your own. (2 Samuel 12 v 9)

After Nathan's rebuke, David repented, and God forgave his sin. David's relationship with the Lord was restored and he returned to following him wholeheartedly. But key to this repentance and restoration was a friend who spoke the truth in love.

There are a few things we can learn from Nathan's conversation with David.

First, Nathan spoke because God told him to. He listened and obeyed God's voice, not his own feelings.

This is what the LORD, the God of Israel, says... (v 7)

It is not usual for you and I to have such a direct and detailed message from the Lord, but sometimes he does prompt us to speak the truth to our neighbour for the purpose of addressing sin and bringing restoration and healing. When he does, will we be obedient? Nathan didn't let his relationship with David or his fear of offending him overshadow the need for confrontation. He was willing to speak the truth because he feared God more than people.

Second, Nathan didn't go in forcefully, shouting at David about everything he had done wrong. Instead, he told a story.

> *There were two men in a certain town, one rich and the other poor. The rich man had a very large number of sheep and cattle, but the poor man had nothing except one little ewe lamb that he had bought. He raised it, and it grew up with him and his children. It shared his food, drank from his cup and even slept in his arms. It was like a daughter to him.*
> *(2 Samuel 12 v 1-3)*

The details Nathan gives about the poor man enable David to empathise with him. He gets a sense of the man's need and his love for his lamb. He is prepared to be horrified by what happens next in the story.

> *Now a traveller came to the rich man, but the rich man refrained from taking one of his own sheep or cattle to prepare a meal for the traveller who had come to him. Instead, he took the ewe lamb that belonged to the poor man and prepared it for the one who had come to him. (v 4)*

It's easy to identify the injustice and cruelty of the rich man towards this poor man we are already feeling compassion for. The story exposes greed, selfishness and disregard for another person. No wonder David reacts as he does.

> *David burned with anger against the man and said to Nathan, "As surely as the LORD lives, the man who did this must die! He must pay for that lamb four times over, because he did such a thing and had no pity." (v 5-6)*

It is only then that Nathan confronts David with his own sin.

> *Then Nathan said to David, "You are the man!" (v 7)*

Nathan's approach was wise. Rarely can we see our own sin as clearly as we should. Often, we need help to understand how our behaviour has offended God and dishonoured others. David had chosen to sweep his sin under the carpet. He had tried to carry on as if he'd done nothing wrong. His heart was hardened, so he may not have responded well to Nathan confronting him directly. But the parable Nathan told enabled David to see his sin clearly and to feel the weight of his wrongdoing.

If you need to confront a brother or sister about their sin, you also need to choose your words wisely. It is rarely helpful to list all the things they have done wrong and demand repentance; your goal is not to shame but to help. You may want to ask questions that gently lead them to see how their behaviour has offended God and hurt others. Or you may share how the Lord has challenged you about similar sins in the past, and how he has helped you change. There may be a story in the Bible that relates to their situation. You could suggest reading it together and talking about how it connects to your own lives. Whatever approach you take, your purpose is to gently help your friend feel the weight of their sin—not so they feel crushed by it, but so they will repent and receive forgiveness.

Third, Nathan's truth-telling resulted not just in repentance but in restoration.

> *Then David said to Nathan, "I have sinned against the LORD." Nathan replied, "The LORD has taken away your sin. You are not going to die." (v 13)*

When confronted so clearly with his sin, David's response was immediate repentance. And God's response was immediate forgiveness. Under the Law of Moses, the penalty for adultery was death—perhaps this is why David tried so hard to conceal his sin. But God shows mercy. He takes away David's sin so that he does not need to be punished for it. Nathan was the instrument God used to confront David with the truth of his sin, but he was also the instrument God used to comfort David with the truth of God's mercy. We can pray that God will use us in the same way—and ponder what restoration and healing will look like for the person we are speaking to, before we decide exactly what we'll say.

Of course, we need to realise that restoration will not always come. You may find that when you speak the truth about something that has happened, whether to you or to someone else, you meet with denials or even a renewal of the sinful behaviour. When this happens, be comforted in knowing that the Lord loves those who speak truth (Psalm 15 v 1-2) and that, in the end, he will deal with all injustice (Proverbs 22 v 8). You are not alone.

THE BRAVERY OF TRUTH

Speaking the truth for the purpose of spiritual growth does not come naturally to most of us. Can you think of times when you have known that the right (and most loving) thing would be to speak the truth, but you have chosen instead to be silent? I can think of times when I have avoided speaking the truth to people who needed correction—a friend who was making choices that would pull her away from the church, a woman who gossiped about a member of her small group, or someone recommending resources that were biblically unfaithful. I can also think of times when I have avoided speaking the truth on behalf of people who needed protection—people in my community whose viewpoints were ignored: unborn babies, people with disabilities who were not being treated with the dignity they deserved.

It's easy to make excuses. *I can't speak for everyone,* I might argue. *And wise people are slow to speak.* But sometimes, to be silent is the least loving thing we can do. When a friend is running towards danger, it is unloving to keep quiet. When someone is mistreated or misrepresented, it is cowardly to say nothing. Doctor Martin Luther King articulated this when he spoke about the number of Americans who refused to stand up against the discrimination of black people and their civil rights: "In the end, we will remember not the words of our enemies, but the silence of our friends" (*The Trumpet of Conscience*, Steeler Lecture, November 1967). In these contexts, speaking the truth is love.

When do you fear speaking the truth? Is it when you risk losing someone's approval? Or when it might result in awkwardness or tension? Is it simply when you're tired and can't face a potentially long and exhausting conversation? My answer is *yes* to all of these reasons. When we feel like this, we need to ask the Spirit to give us power over our idols of comfort, approval and control; love for those we should speak to; and wisdom to know what to say. We can be confident he will answer because Jesus promised that the Spirit of truth will guide us into all truth (John 16 v 13).

We should not be surprised when it feels hard. Before God brought us into his family, we belonged to the devil and followed his ways. Jesus calls him "a liar and the father of lies" (John 8 v 44). So truth is not our first language—lies, exaggeration, flattery, manipulation, blame-shifting and glory-stealing are. But Jesus teaches us to know the truth that frees us to speak like him.

A TRUER STORY

For many years after I became a Christian, I thought that speaking the truth meant not telling lies. I knew the ninth commandment: "You shall not give false testimony against your neighbour" (Exodus 20 v 16). But I didn't understand that God has a far more positive vision for our speech than that. He calls us not simply to avoid lies, but to proactively speak the truth of his word to one another. He calls us to remind one another of the truth that we have been rescued from Satan's kingdom and brought into the kingdom of God's Son (Colossians 1 v 13); that we have a glorious inheritance to look forward to (1 Peter 1 v 3-5); and that he is transforming us to become more like Jesus (2 Corinthians 3 v 18). We can all speak the truth in this way. It is not only about confronting sin and injustice. It is about speaking the truth every day as we encourage one another with God's word and remind each other of the truer story we are part of.

Think about your church family. Who could you encourage this week with the truth that they are forgiven and accepted by their heavenly Father? Who would be strengthened by the reminder that this world is not all there is and that life in the new creation will be full of joy and peace? Who may be feeling despondent about their slow growth in godliness? Perhaps there's someone you could call or message, even today, to remind them that God will continue the work he has begun in them and bring it to completion (Philippians 1 v 6).

Jesus calls us to teach and admonish one another, and to speak to one another with psalms, hymns and songs from the Spirit (Ephesians 5 v 19; Colossians 3 v 16). That's a far more beautiful vision for our speech than simply avoiding lies.

QUESTIONS FOR REFLECTION

1. *When are you most tempted not to speak the truth? What do you fear in those situations?*

2. *What difference should it make to the way we speak truth to other believers when we remember that we are all members of Christ's body?*

3. *What most strikes you about the way Nathan speaks truth to David? How might considering the motive, method and possible results help you in a situation where you need to confront sin?*

4. *Paul says, "Speaking the truth in love, we will grow to become in every respect the mature body of him who is the head" (Ephesians 4 v 15). Can you think of a specific way in which you could help someone in your church family grow in faith by speaking truth to them this week?*

A CELLO IN THE DARK

SPEAKING BEAUTY

Whatever is true, whatever is noble, whatever is right, whatever is pure, whatever is lovely, whatever is admirable—if anything is excellent or praiseworthy— think about such things.

Philippians 4 v 8

I wonder if the world feels beautiful to you.

It's very easy for it not to. The soundtrack of our world is loud and relentless, isn't it? It is hard to escape the pulsing beat of *Do better, Work harder, Strive for success, Be the best*. Listening to that can be exhausting and disheartening. What if we can't do better? What if we work hard but still miss the mark? There isn't time to consider beauty in the midst of so much striving. Then there are the melancholic songs of global tragedy, civil unrest, and wide-scale suffering which pull us towards fear and despair each time we turn on the news or scroll our social-media feeds. Criticism, gossip, cynicism and negativity accompany us as we work, rest, and even worship. We may wish we could turn off the music, but instead we find ourselves singing along.

But it's possible to sing a different song.

The siege of Sarajevo is the longest siege recorded in modern history. From April 1992 to February 1996, thousands of its citizens were killed as the city faced relentless attacks from surrounding forces. Apartments, marketplaces and schools were destroyed, and the city was left without electricity, gas, water, transport or industry. Yet amid the ugliness and chaos of war, one man sought to bring beauty into view. Vedran Smailović, a cellist from Bosnia and Herzegovina, sat in the ruined streets and buildings and played his cello for the grieving, fearful people of Sarajevo. For two years he played at different locations around the city. He reminded his neighbours that beauty could still be seen and heard—even amid great suffering. He brought hope and healing.

As followers of Jesus, we are called to sing a new song. We cannot—and should not—ignore the ugliness of the world; but, like Vedran Smailović, we *can* interrupt its soundtrack with a more beautiful song.

In chapter 2 we thought about speaking truth. In this chapter, we are going to consider how we learn to speak about things that are beautiful and good. There is overlap between the two—philosophers have argued for centuries that there is no real beauty or goodness without truth. But I wonder if, out of a right desire to defend and promote the truth, many Christians overlook the importance of thinking and speaking about all that is beautiful. Perhaps you have never thought about the importance of beauty in your speech. I hope this chapter will help you think differently.

LEARN FROM THE LILIES

It is hard to define beauty, but we know it when we see it—or hear it, smell it, touch it or taste it. Beauty elicits some kind of response in us, even if it is just to exclaim, "Wow!" A stunning sunset, a haunting piece of music, soft silk, fragrant flowers, the perfect raspberry panna cotta. As I write, I am distracted by the subtle hints of plum blossom in a scented candle a friend bought for me, and the striking magenta petals of the carnations in a vase on my kitchen table.

God has made a world full of beauty, and while it is true that parts of it have been spoiled by sin, there is so much beauty that remains if we will take the time to look for it. The problem is, we often don't. It is easier to focus on the negative—what went wrong in our day, what someone said that was unkind, a difficult relationship; disappointments, discouragements and regrets.

But as those who know the one who is the source of all beauty and the one to whom all beauty points, we should be on the lookout for every hint of beauty we can find. Christian writer Dallas Willard once said, "Beauty is God's goodness made manifest to the senses" (conversatio. org/discipleship-as-life-in-the-kingdom). When we see, hear, touch, taste or smell things that provoke a "Wow!" response, we experience something of God's goodness, and it should change our perspective—just like the beautiful music of Vedran Smailović.

In Luke 12, Jesus speaks to his followers about things we all recognise as beautiful—the natural world. But he doesn't speak about beautiful things just for the sake of it. He wants to change his followers' perspective. He wants the beauty they experience to orient their hearts to the God who reveals himself through it.

> *Consider how the wild flowers grow. They do not labour or spin. Yet I tell you, not even Solomon in all his splendour was dressed like one of these. If that is how God clothes the grass of the field, which is here today, and tomorrow is thrown into the fire, how much more will he clothe you—you of little faith!*
> *(Luke 12 v 27-28)*

In springtime, the fields of Palestine are covered with poppies, daisies, anemones, tulips, cyclamen, irises, lupins, marigolds and a host of other beautiful flowers. These flowers are not planted or watered by horticulturists, and they do not look after themselves. And yet their beauty rivals the finely woven robes of Israel's wealthiest king! But while these beautiful flowers should be admired and enjoyed, they also teach an important lesson about God's care for his people. If he provides such beautiful clothing for flowers that last only a few days before fading and dying (Isaiah 40 v 7), he will certainly care for his children who will live and praise him for ever. Jesus uses the beauty of the natural world to reorient his listeners' hearts from worry about not having enough to dependent trust in the God who knows their needs and will provide for them.

And do not set your heart on what you will eat or drink; do not worry about it. For the pagan world runs after all such things, and your Father knows that you need them. But seek his kingdom, and these things will be given to you as well. (Luke 12 v 29-31)

The beauty of creation reminds Jesus' followers that they have a heavenly Father who is both powerful and loving. He is able to take care of them—and he delights to do so. This means that they do not need to worry about the things unbelievers worry about, but are free to pursue something far greater: God's kingdom.

This is not the only occasion when Jesus highlighted beauty to make his point. He often referred to the natural world (e.g. Matthew 13 v 3-9; Mark 4 v 26-32; Luke 6 v 43-44), and he drew attention to beautiful acts of devotion (Mark 12 v 41-44; 14 v 6). It is effective because beauty affects us emotionally in a way that abstract concepts rarely do. It is therefore more likely to impact our thinking and behaviour. And this is what we, too, can hope for as we speak about all that is beautiful and good.

A BETTER STORY

In Philippians 4 v 8, Paul tells believers to think about whatever is true, noble, right, pure, lovely, and admirable. He summarises, "If anything is excellent or praiseworthy—think about such things". He knows how easy it is to focus on things that are not excellent or praiseworthy. Things that are false, dishonourable, unjust, impure, ugly and unworthy of our attention. Things that cause us to doubt God's goodness and propel us towards unbelief and ungodliness. But pulling our thoughts back to that which is excellent and praiseworthy will correct false thinking and restore our joy.

When we lose sight of beauty, we quickly become weary, bored and disillusioned. Life loses its lustre. But beauty reawakens us and inspires fresh hope. When we feel overwhelmed by the brokenness of the world, focusing on what is pure, lovely and admirable renews our perspective and draws us back to the story of redemption. It reminds us that the new creation has already begun, and one day God will finish remaking all that is broken. When we hear stories of forgiveness and reconciliation, we dare to believe that our own difficult relationships—or those of people we love—may one day be restored. When we witness strangers offering shelter and support for refugees or victims of natural disaster, cynicism is replaced by the courage to engage in our own small acts of kindness.

It is easy to ignore these beautiful things and to fill our speech with worries and cynicism. To focus on all that is wrong in the world, rather than what is good. To over-think and over-share every fear. But filling our speech with worries and cynicism rarely helps us—or those we speak to. If anything, it strengthens negative feelings and makes things worse.

As Christians we know there is a better story and there are more beautiful things to say. In the ordinary moments of each day, we can bring beauty into view by training ourselves to look for the things that reveal God's goodness—and then sharing them with others. That does not mean we avoid talking about anything that is ugly and broken. It is right that we expose evil in our world, and we should express sadness and anger at it. But we can delight in knowing that God's goodness is even greater, and take every opportunity to draw attention to that.

This is what David does in Psalm 23, for example. He is realistic about the ugliness in the world—he faces up to evil (v 4), enemies (v 5), and even death (v 4). But beauty—the tangible experience of God's goodness—enables him to view these things with a hopeful perspective. David identifies with a sheep—safe and secure in the care of the Good Shepherd. He is aware of the Lord's provision and protection as he gives him rest in "green pastures" (v 2), leads him "beside quiet waters" (v 2), and guides him along the right paths (v 3). Even as he walks through darkness, he is unafraid because he is aware of the Shepherd's presence (v 4) and the comfort of his rod and staff.

In verse 5, he describes a banquet table, anointing oil and a cup overflowing with blessing—beautiful, earthy images that pull his heart away from fear and towards the Lord. He is aware of God's beauty and love pursuing him and leading him to his eternal home.

Your beauty and love chase after me
every day of my life.
I'm back home in the house of GOD
for the rest of my life. (v 6, The Message)

David delights in beauty, and allows it to redirect his focus from the temporal to the transcendent. He sees hints of goodness and beauty shining through evil and ugliness. And he is confident in God's power to take what is ugly and broken and make it truly beautiful. This should be the perspective we share with those we speak to.

The best place to see the transformation of an ugly situation into one of pure beauty is at the cross. A greedy friend's betrayal led to Jesus' arrest in the Garden of Gethsemane. At the home of the high priest, guards mocked and beat Jesus, while, outside in the courtyard, another close friend denied ever knowing him. Lies and false accusations followed him from the high priest's house to the governor's palace and through the dusty streets of Jerusalem to the hill where Jesus was crucified. Around his cross, crowds watched while leaders scoffed, soldiers taunted, and a criminal hanging next to him yelled insults. It looked and sounded like the ugliest of situations—a place where beauty was completely hidden. And yet it wasn't.

As he was crucified, Jesus spoke the most beautiful words, "Father, forgive them, for they do not know what they are doing" (Luke 23 v 34). Compassion and love flowed as he prayed for his enemies, provided for his mother (John 19 v 26-27), and promised eternal life to the thief dying beside him (Luke 23 v 43). His humility overshadowed the soldiers' brutality as he refused to retaliate to their insults or threaten revenge (1 Peter 2 v 23). Against a backdrop of violence and hatred, Jesus' grace was in full view as he gave himself up as a willing sacrifice for sin, so that we could be forgiven, made holy and reconciled to God (Ephesians 5 v 2; Colossians 1 v 22).

Often the most breathtaking beauty is that which is unexpected. No one in 1st-century Jerusalem would have imagined that anything of beauty could be forged by an instrument of Roman torture. But the nail marks on Jesus' resurrected body testify that evil has been dealt with, the powers of darkness are defeated and, one day, life on Earth will be perfect. If we can see such beauty in such ugliness at the cross, then we can also see beauty in the ugliest situations we face in our own lives.

FINDING BEAUTY

It is not easy to focus our speech on all that is excellent and praiseworthy while we are surrounded by much that is not. When life is hard, and especially in seasons of suffering, we may wonder what we can say that is beautiful and beneficial. How do we train ourselves to notice—and speak about—the things that are true, right, noble, pure, lovely and admirable when the things that are up close and personal seem ugly and useless?

Paul wrote his letter to the Philippians while he was in chains. He understood as well as anyone that life is not always easy. In fact, his own story was one of great suffering. In another letter he writes:

> *Five times I received from the Jews the forty lashes minus one. Three times I was beaten with rods, once I was pelted with stones, three times I was shipwrecked, I spent a night and a day in the open sea, I have been constantly on the move. I have been in danger from rivers, in danger from bandits, in danger from my fellow Jews, in danger from Gentiles; in danger in*

*the city, in danger in the country, in danger at sea;
and in danger from false believers. I have laboured
and toiled and have often gone without sleep; I have
known hunger and thirst and have often gone without
food; I have been cold and naked. Besides everything
else, I face daily the pressure of my concern for all the
churches. (2 Corinthians 11 v 24-28)*

Paul experienced extreme hardship, yet his letter to the
Philippians is characterised by joy. As he writes from
chains, uncertain whether he faces release or death, he
models what it looks like to see God's goodness in times of
difficulty and to point others to him. You and I are unlikely
to suffer in the way Paul did, but we will inevitably experience pain and suffering in our lives. Will we look for God's
goodness and share it with those around us?

Perhaps you are suffering a long-term illness or grieving
a loss. How is the Lord sustaining you? Is there a Bible
verse or passage that brings you comfort and hope? Who
could you share this with? At a church prayer meeting
earlier this week, a friend asked us to give thanks for
the ways God has shown his kindness to her since her
husband died a few months ago. As she spoke, we were
reminded of God's compassion and care, and we praised
him together. I am grateful that this friend didn't keep
quiet but chose to speak about the grace she experiences
even in grief. Her words have inspired me to praise God
for his kindness to her, and to look for evidence of his
grace in my own life.

Even amid brokenness, there is beauty to be found if we
will look for it. In fact, many of the most beautiful things

grow out of what was most broken. It may be tempting to put the search for beauty on hold until we are in a better season, but choosing to acknowledge God's goodness in times of difficulty both glorifies him and increases our joy.

A few years ago, a close friend of mine died after a 20-month-long battle with cancer. During the last few months of her life she suffered excruciating physical pain, alongside the grief of knowing that her children would grow up without their mother. But in her suffering, she learned to sing a new song. Every day she repeated its chorus to herself, her family and her friends: *God is good. God is wise. God is loving.* It was beautiful, comforting and inspiring to hear her tell a truer story than the one her body declared.

SPEAKING BEAUTY

Whatever our circumstances, we can learn to look for the things that are excellent and praiseworthy, and share them with those around us. But it will take some effort to make this a habit—and we will probably have to work hard to correct ingrained speech habits that are not beautiful.

When our guard is down, it is easy to be drawn into gossip, criticism and complaining. Or to slip back into speech habits that characterised our old way of life: anger, rage, malice, slander, filthy language and lies (Colossians 3 v 8-9); obscenity, foolish talk or coarse joking (Ephesians 5 v 4). The ugliness of the world can invade our speech through sarcasm, teasing, belittling or shaming that make people feel bad about themselves. If we are not careful, even well-intentioned teasing and banter can cut down rather than build up those we are called to love.

Perhaps you struggle with pessimism and imagine the worst in situations or people. Instead of allowing your conversation to be characterised by negativity, try to work harder at looking for what is positive and talk about that. When you talk about the people in your life, make a point of saying what you appreciate about them—what is admirable—rather than what drives you mad. Be quick to praise and affirm rather than criticise and complain (we will think about this more in chapter 7).

If your co-workers are gossiping about another colleague, don't join in. Instead, try to highlight that colleague's strengths or achievements. Or, if you can't think of any, politely excuse yourself and walk away. When you are talking with family or friends, don't exaggerate failures or weaknesses (your own or those of others), but try to emphasise what is virtuous, just or kind. If they are believers, talk about the marks of spiritual growth you see in one another. Don't be drawn into insincere flattery but look to genuinely encourage each other to keep growing in godliness.

And when you are discouraged by the ugliness that often dominates news and social-media feeds, stop scrolling and pray. Ask God to bring justice and peace. Ask him to show you practical ways in which you may be able to help those who suffer. And then try to remember where you have recently experienced his goodness through beauty.

A GREATER TREASURE

As we have already seen, ultimate beauty is seen in Jesus. He is where we see God's goodness most clearly on display. To those who belong to him, there is nothing more beautiful than the resurrection of Jesus Christ from the dead and the promise of eternal life with him. This is what Jesus wants his followers to focus on as they live in this present world with all its trouble and worry. In Luke 12, he redirects the disciples' focus from fear about not having enough in this life to the eternal treasure of heaven. After speaking about the wild flowers he says:

> *Do not be afraid, little flock, for your Father has been pleased to give you the kingdom. Sell your possessions and give to the poor. Provide purses for yourselves that will not wear out, a treasure in heaven that will never fail, where no thief comes near and no moth destroys. For where your treasure is, there your heart will be also. (Luke 12 v 32-34)*

Jesus reassures his disciples that their heavenly Father is pleased to include them in his kingdom. Because of that, they can obey his commands to be generous and care for others, knowing that as they do so they are storing up an eternal reward that is far greater than any earthly treasure.

Jesus doesn't lecture but uses beautiful imagery that will draw the disciples into the good news of the gospel. Like us, they are tempted to view life only from an earthly perspective. But Jesus reminds them of the truer, better story they are part of. He lifts their gaze from earthly concerns and reorients their hearts towards eternal treasure. And this is what our words can do, too. In every conversation, we have an opportunity to remind each other of the beauty of the gospel. To encourage one another to look beyond what is in view to what is eternal. And to reorient ourselves to the one who is most excellent and worthy of all praise.

QUESTIONS FOR REFLECTION

1. *When do you most often find yourself listening to the world's soundtrack? How does it impact your feelings, your habits and your words?*

2. *How could you start training yourself to look for things that reveal God's goodness? What difference do you think this might make to your everyday conversations—in person and online?*

3. *Can you think of an ugly situation that God has used to reveal more of his goodness through? How does this give you hope in the face of suffering and bad news stories?*

4. *David says, "Your beauty and love chase after me every day of my life" (Psalm 23 v 6, The Message). Where do you see God's beauty chasing you today? How will you use your words to encourage others to look to him?*

FROM THE FATHER OF COMPASSION

SPEAKING COMFORT

Praise be to the God and Father of our Lord Jesus Christ, the Father of compassion and the God of all comfort, who comforts us in all our troubles, so that we can comfort those in any trouble with the comfort we ourselves receive from God.

2 Corinthians 1 v 3-4

She died on Easter Sunday. Her husband, widowed after 63 years of marriage, sobbed as he sat by her bed trying to imagine life without her. The family gathered round, each filled with grief, shock and overwhelming sorrow. What words could bring comfort at such a time of loss?

His short life had brought unexpected joy to his parents, and they were thankful for 186 days of knowing and caring for him. It was more than they had dared to hope for, yet they were unprepared for the crushing pain of saying goodbye. Could any words bring consolation in the face of such anguish?

Twenty-one years ago, they promised to love each other until death. But today, she sits alone. His words have crushed her spirit and broken her heart. Could the words of a friend relieve feelings of worthlessness and betrayal?

These are all real people—people I know. As each of them suffered and grieved, I desperately wanted to speak words of comfort and consolation. And I was painfully aware of how easy it is to say something tactless or hurtful without intending to. Sometimes we speak without thinking and later regret our words. On other occasions, we are so afraid of saying the wrong thing that, instead, we say nothing at all.

Even if we have known comfort in hard times ourselves, it can be difficult in the moment to know just what to say that will help those who are suffering and not add to their pain. We don't want to offer trite words that fill a silence but do nothing to console a broken heart. And we don't want to offer false comfort. No, we want our words to bring real comfort to those who are hurting. But is this something we can ever get right?

2 Corinthians 1 v 3-4 tells us it *is* possible to comfort people well—because we have God's comfort. Paul reminds us that God is the God of all comfort who comforts those who are suffering. But one of the ways he does this is through his people. He uses us to comfort others with the comfort we have received in our own times of suffering. It's an amazing thought: when we comfort people with God's comfort, there can be no trite

or empty words, only truth and power. Our compassionate God works through us to bring help and healing to those who need it most. And he promises that this is possible in all and any trouble.

What will it look like for you and I to speak such words? If we want to comfort people with God's comfort, we first need to understand what kind of comfort God gives. So we're going to look at one of the great comfort speeches of the Old Testament.

COMFORT MY PEOPLE

In Isaiah 40, God's spokesperson brings a message of hope to people facing the trauma of exile. The northern kingdom, Israel, has already been conquered by the nation of Assyria, and the southern kingdom, Judah, will soon be overthrown by the powerful Babylonians. Isaiah has spoken words of warning and judgment for 39 chapters, but in chapter 40, his tone and his message shift as, through him, God speaks hope to his discouraged people.

> *Comfort, comfort my people,*
> *says your God.*
> *Speak tenderly to Jerusalem,*
> *and proclaim to her*
> *that her hard service has been completed,*
> *that her sin has been paid for,*
> *that she has received from the* LORD's *hand*
> *double for all her sins. (Isaiah 40 v 1-2)*

When you or I think about offering comfort, we usually think of trying to ease someone's pain and make them feel better. But the Hebrew word is stronger. It means to strengthen and give courage, to help make secure. So God is telling Isaiah to give his people courage as they face enemies and exile. He tells them not to despair because he will deliver them. They will suffer, but God will not abandon them. He will fulfil his promises and showcase his glory to the nations through them.

The purpose of Isaiah's message is to give God's people the strength they need to persevere until the day of deliverance. And that is our purpose in speaking comfort too. We want to encourage those who suffer to persevere and trust in God's good purposes for them as they wait for him to deliver them from their trials—whether that happens in this life or in eternity.

God tells Isaiah to speak tenderly to his people. They have sinned against him, but he is compassionate. They are weighed down by the burden of their sin, but one day he will lift that burden from them. They will be punished for their sin as they go into exile in Babylon, but their punishment will not be as great as their sin deserves. Ultimately, their sin will be atoned for by the servant described in Isaiah's following chapters—a servant who will come and receive the punishment on their behalf.

When my friend Elaine was dying of bowel cancer, she would tell people that her greatest burden was not her cancer but her sin; and so her greatest comfort was not relief from pain or the hope of successful treatment, but the knowledge that her sin had been forgiven for ever. That through the life, death, resurrection and ascension of Jesus, she was assured of eternal life in a resurrected body on a renewed earth in a perfectly restored relationship with her God. This is the greatest comfort anyone could know in this life. And this is the comfort we *can* know if we are trusting in Christ.

I am not saying that other burdens are not significant or that we shouldn't seek to offer comfort for illness, bereavement, or broken relationships. But the comfort all of us primarily need is the comfort of forgiveness. That is the foundation on which we seek to provide comfort for other trials.

If a Christian friend loses her job and is struggling to trust God to meet her financial needs, we might gently remind her that because God was willing to give up his own Son to meet her need of forgiveness, she can trust him to provide for her other needs too (Romans 8 v 32). If a friend with chronic ill health asks why God has allowed him to suffer in this way, we can't pretend to know the exact reasons God has ordained his particular suffering, but we can remind him that, since his sin is forgiven, he can persevere with hope because of the resurrection life that is to come. And we can pray that, like Elaine, he will find that to be truly comforting.

We don't, however, want to offer false comfort. For example, if someone is experiencing guilt over their part in a broken relationship, it may be tempting to try to assure them that they are not to blame for what has happened. But perhaps they are—at least to some degree. What we can do is assure them that, even if they are unable to reconcile with the person they have hurt, if they confess their wrongdoing to God and ask for his forgiveness, he is willing to give it. Similarly, to assure someone that God loves and accepts them as they are when we know they are not trusting in Christ is false comfort. What we can do is tell them about the acceptance we have found with God through Christ, and encourage them to come to him for forgiveness and love. (We will think about this more in chapter 6.)

BEHOLD YOUR GOD!

God's message of comfort starts with the assurance of his forgiveness. It is enforced by a reminder of his character. Isaiah is to lift his voice and declare to the cities of Judah, "Behold your God!" (v 9, ESV).

When we suffer, our problems can seem very big, and God can appear very small. So we need to realign our vision so that we see him as he is: powerful, wise and loving. This is what will help us to persevere in trusting him when life is painful or perplexing. And this is what we must help our suffering friends to do too. We bring comfort by bringing into focus the character of our God.

In Isaiah 40, God comforts his people by reminding them, firstly, that he is supremely powerful.

See, the Sovereign LORD comes with power,
and he rules with a mighty arm. (v 10)

Our God is the powerful one who created the world with a word. He speaks and darkness turns to light (Genesis 1 v 3). He measures the oceans in the hollow of his hand and the heavens with its breadth (Isaiah 40 v 12). He holds the dust of the earth in a basket, and weighs the mountains in his scales (v 12). He picks up the earth as though it were a grain of sand (v 15, NLT). His word endures for ever (v 8).

We can comfort our friends with this truth: their problems may be great and their circumstances overwhelming, but their God is powerful and he can deliver them. The one who makes sure not even one star is missing from its place in the heavens (v 26) will surely look after his people.

Secondly, God comforts his people by reminding them that he is incomparably wise.

> *Who can fathom the Spirit of the LORD,*
> *   or instruct the LORD as his counsellor?*
> *Whom did the LORD consult to enlighten him,*
> *   and who taught him the right way?*
> *Who was it that taught him knowledge,*
> *   or showed him the path of understanding?*
>
> *(v 13-14)*

God's people thought they would be destroyed for ever when their city fell into the hands of their enemies. They did not believe that God would raise them up again. "My way is hidden from the LORD; my cause is disregarded by my God", they complained (v 27). But although they could see no way home from exile, God did. He would make a straight highway right through the middle of the desert (v 3).

God was not surprised by the suffering of his people. Their problems were not too complex for him to straighten out. He not only has the power to deliver, but the wisdom to know how.

Do you not know?
  Have you not heard?
The LORD is the everlasting God,
  the Creator of the ends of the earth.
He will not grow tired or weary,
  and his understanding no one can fathom. (v 28)

God's strength is matched by his wisdom. He sees every detail of our lives, and he knows exactly how to work for our good in every circumstance.

This is not true of you and me. We cannot fully understand what God is doing—whether in our own lives or in the lives of those we seek to support. So when we want to comfort those who are suffering, it's not helpful to pretend we know more than we really do. But we *can* remind our friends that their heavenly Father is all-knowing and all-wise. There is no circumstance he does not understand, no problem he is unable to solve, no relationship he is unable to fix, no pain he is unable to heal. Every detail of their lives is fully known and understood by him.

Thirdly, God comforts his people by reminding them that he is infinitely loving.

He tends his flock like a shepherd:
  he gathers the lambs in his arms
and carries them close to his heart;
  he gently leads those that have young. (v 11)

Despite Israel's rebellion against him, the Lord is loving and tender towards his people. He is a mighty God and a compassionate Father. He speaks tenderly to his people despite their sin (v 2). He will use his power and might to rescue and restore them.

We can comfort our suffering friends by assuring them that God is not distant or uninterested in their suffering, but is compassionate and concerned for their good. He will care for them and carry them through all their struggles and sorrows.

If a friend feels weak and over-burdened, we can remind them that God never grows tired or weary. Rather, he gives *his* strength to the weary and increases the power of the weak (v 29). When someone is bewildered by troubling circumstances, we can tell them that, while we don't understand either, God does. And we can pray that he will give them wisdom as they persevere in their trial. As we talk with people experiencing grief and heartache, we can point them to our loving Shepherd who carries them close to his heart.

God spoke these words of comfort into a specific situation, but his promises are relevant to us all. The deliverance he promised then is the same deliverance he has promised to us. Of course, the people of Judah could not see how God would accomplish this deliverance—they saw only their defeat. But 700 years later, Isaiah's words of comfort would ring out again as John the Baptist travelled around the region of the River Jordan announcing:

Every valley shall be filled in,
  every mountain and hill made low.
The crooked roads shall become straight,
  the rough ways smooth.
And all people will see God's salvation. (Luke 3 v 5-6)

Then Jesus came—filled with power, wisdom and compassion (Luke 4 v 14; Luke 2 v 40; Mark 6 v 34). The God of all comfort entered our world to share our sorrows and bear our burdens.

We will think more about Jesus' comfort in a moment—but first, it may be helpful to stop reading for a moment to reflect and pray. Who are you seeking to comfort? What will it look like for you to comfort them with God's comfort—with the knowledge that he forgives sin, and that he is supremely powerful, incomparably wise, and infinitely loving? This will be easier if your friend is a Christian, but there may be something here you could say to a non-Christian friend too, in a gentle way that points them to Jesus. Read through Isaiah 40 for yourself and ask the Lord to show you what words would be most helpful for your suffering or grieving friend.

GLORY THROUGH SUFFERING

The death of Martha's brother had left her desolate, vulnerable and confused. She had sent word when he became ill, but her friend hadn't come. She knew he was powerful—she had seen him heal others. And she knew he loved her family so she had thought he would come straight away. But he didn't.

By the time Jesus arrived, it was too late—Martha's brother had been dead four days. They had wrapped him in grave clothes and buried him in a tomb. Friends and neighbours gathered to comfort Martha and her sister, but the one person she really wanted was missing.

When word finally came that Jesus was near the village,

Martha left her sister with the wailers and well-wishers, and went out to meet him.

> *"Lord," Martha said to Jesus, "if you had been here, my brother would not have died."*
>
> *"Your brother will rise again."*
>
> *"I know he will rise again in the resurrection at the last day."*
>
> *Jesus said to her, "I am the resurrection and the life. The one who believes in me will live, even though they die; and whoever lives by believing in me will never die. Do you believe this?"*
>
> *(from John 11 v 21-26)*

Jesus offers Martha comfort that the mourners at her home could not. He tells her that death will not have the last word.

To begin with, Jesus echoes words Martha would probably have heard from devout Jews visiting her home—her brother's body will be restored at the resurrection on the last day. But Jesus wants to redirect Martha's focus from an intellectual belief in the resurrection to a personal belief in the one who guarantees that hope—the one who will not only raise the dead but who is himself the resurrection and the life.

How does this truth comfort those who suffer today? Jesus no longer walks on Earth healing the sick and raising the dead. He proved that he is God by raising Lazarus (John 11 v 42-44), but how does that comfort a chronic-fatigue sufferer today who still cannot walk or work?

Or a grieving widow whose husband will not wake up? Or the parents of a drug-addicted teenager? Or the child of an abusive parent? What difference does it make *now* that Jesus is the resurrection and the life?

Here's one answer. John tells us that Jesus delayed his journey to Martha's home because he loved her and her family (v 5-6). If he hadn't raised Lazarus from the dead, that would make no sense—the loving response would be to heal Lazarus and spare his sisters grief. But we can now see that it was more loving to let Lazarus die and let them grieve for a short time so that they could experience more of his glory. Jesus shows his love for them by revealing more of who he is. He shows his power, wisdom and love in ways they could not experience without first suffering.

So it is with believers who suffer today. Jesus does not show his love to us by sparing us suffering, but by giving us himself and showing us his glory *through* our suffering.

Joni Eareckson Tada has been a quadriplegic for over 50 years. In an article in 2017, she wrote the following:

> *It sounds incredible, but I really would rather be in this wheelchair knowing Jesus as I do than be on my feet without him … I can't tell you how many nights I have lain in bed, unable to move, stiff with pain, and have whispered near tears, "Oh, Jesus, I'm so happy. So very happy in you!" I thank God every day for my wheelchair.*
>
> *(www.thegospelcoalition.com, 30 July 2017)*

Not every believer will experience Christ's presence and joy in the way Joni has. And we must be careful not to pressure one another to respond to suffering in exactly the same way. But her testimony is an encouragement that Jesus uses suffering to show his power, wisdom and love in unique ways. We can comfort one another with the truth that Jesus' glory and love are shown most clearly to us when we are weak and in need.

IT'S NOT ABOUT YOU

As we seek to comfort suffering believers, our goal is to direct their focus to Christ and the hope of eternal life and joy in him. But we want to do this in a way that doesn't minimise their present pain. You and I cannot speak with the same authority and compassion that Jesus spoke with. We are unable to fully understand someone's grief or change their difficult circumstances—and we shouldn't pretend we can.

In her book *What Grieving People Wish You Knew* (p 24), Nancy Guthrie writes, "Grieving people are not expecting you to make the pain go away. They're really just hoping that you will be willing to hurt with them." Doesn't that relieve the pressure we often feel to fix things? You and I are unable to mend broken relationships, cure addictions, heal mental illness or raise the dead. But we can come alongside those who suffer and agree that what they're experiencing is heartbreaking and inexplicable. We can express sorrow over their suffering. We can "weep with those who weep" (Romans 12 v 15, ESV).

Even if we have experienced a similar loss or pain, we cannot know exactly how another person is feeling. The way we suffer is as unique as the suffering itself. One of my friends struggles with her infertility differently to another—and for different reasons. There are cultural and familial pressures on her because of where she is from, and this impacts her suffering. As well as her personal sense of unfulfilled longing, she faces pressure and criticism from family members who feel she has dishonoured the family name. She suffers public shame as well as personal pain. That doesn't mean her suffering is greater than that of my other friend, but it is different, and I need to be sensitive to each of their unique struggles.

Rather than being quick to identify with another person's suffering, we should listen carefully to what they say. And rather than trying to offer simple solutions, we can acknowledge our lack of understanding. Even if you think you understand, try to hold back until you are asked to share your experience—don't make someone else's suffering about you!

But while we may not be able to identify completely with another person's suffering, we are still able to bring comfort. Paul tells us that we can comfort people in *any* trouble with the comfort we have received from God (2 Corinthians 1 v 4). How is this possible? Because, as we've seen in Isaiah 40, true comfort comes from eternal truth.

We must take care to listen well. We must not presume to know exactly how someone feels, or what they should do. We should enter into the pain of those we are seeking to comfort with humility and gentleness. But we can speak words that are truly comforting because they point to the source of all comfort. (And while we have been focusing in this chapter on comforting Christians, much of this applies to comforting unbelievers too—we just may need to phrase things differently.)

The truths we've read in Isaiah 40 are timeless because the character of our God is unchanging, and his word endures for ever (Isaiah 40 v 8). The comfort we receive in our own trials is the same comfort we can offer others: God is powerful, wise and loving. He has sent us his son Jesus, forgiven our sins and promised to lead us to eternal life.

QUESTIONS FOR REFLECTION

1. *When someone you know is suffering, are you more likely to say too much or say nothing at all? What do you think are your underlying concerns or fears?*

2. *How might focusing on God's character rather than your own experience (or lack of it) help you bring genuine comfort to those who need it?*

3. *Think of some people you know who are struggling in difficult or painful circumstances. What truths from Isaiah 40 could be helpful to each of them? Try to think of specific ways you could share these truths in your conversations.*

4. *Jesus says, "I am the resurrection and the life" (John 11 v 25). Who can you comfort with this truth this week?*

SOMEBODY'S DAUGHTER

SPEAKING KINDNESS

Therefore, as God's chosen people, holy and dearly loved, clothe yourselves with compassion, kindness, humility, gentleness and patience.

Colossians 3 v 12

When Gini Bonnell painted two words and a red heart on an old piece of wood and planted it in her front garden, she could not have imagined that her simple idea to encourage acts of kindness in her neighbourhood would explode into a global movement. But since 2018, Gini's *Be Kind* signs have been copied and recreated throughout the US and further afield. Where I live in the UK, garden signs are not so common but the *Be Kind* message is displayed widely—on posters, mugs, cushions, teaspoons, baseball caps and even dog collars. Today, I am writing at my kitchen table wearing a *Be Kind* sweatshirt!

It is unsurprising that the plea to be kind resonates deeply. We all know how it feels to be on the receiving end of unkind words—impatience, sarcasm, mockery and disparagement. They make us feel small and unvalued. In our culture, kind words are often in short supply. If I voice an opinion that is not shared by the majority, I anticipate a hostile response. On social media, I fear my views will be met with criticism and contempt rather than consideration and respect.

But although it is a helpful prompt to think before responding harshly, the *Be Kind* slogan is just that—a slogan. It doesn't really provide the motivation to change our speech for good. It doesn't get to the heart of what kindness is or what kind speech would sound like. And it doesn't equip us with the power to speak kindly in every situation. There is far more to say about kindness than can be encapsulated in two words.

I wonder what you think when you hear the words *Be Kind*. Perhaps you feel guilty. You try hard to be kind, but often find yourself getting irritable and grumpy. Maybe you feel quite pleased with yourself. You like to think of yourself as being a kind person and imagine others do, too. Or maybe you are frustrated by the whole idea behind the *Be Kind* slogan. Why is everyone so over-sensitive all the time? What's so wrong with just saying what you really think?

This chapter is going to challenge and deepen our understanding of kindness. We often equate kindness with niceness—being pleasant and generally getting along with people. Kind speech, then, would be speech that doesn't hurt feelings or raise hackles. Sweet. Safe.

Inoffensive. But the Bible portrays a much stronger picture, which will motivate and equip us to be kind as well as giving us a deeper understanding of what kindness is—a deliberate reorienting of our hearts towards others, even when they don't deserve it.

AN UNEXPECTED GIFT

In the New Testament, the Greek word most often used for "kind", *chrestos*, has less to do with being sweet or pleasant, and more to do with goodness, gentleness, generosity and grace (Matthew 11 v 30; Luke 6 v 35; Galatians 5 v 22; Ephesians 4 v 32; 1 Peter 2 v 3). It encompasses the kindness of God that we see throughout the Bible as he forgives, rescues and provides for his wayward people. His kindness is the tangible expression of his steadfast love towards people who do not deserve it.

And that's the thing about kindness: it is undeserved. It is not a reward that can be earned, but an unexpected gift. It is not based on fairness—*you'll get from me exactly what you have given and no more*—but is extravagantly generous. God's kindness is inextricably linked to his mercy. He does not treat us as we deserve, but is compassionate and gracious, slow to anger and abounding in love and faithfulness (Exodus 34 v 6).

In Middle English, the word *kind* was linked with the word *kin*. To be kind meant to deliberately choose to do good with the feelings that a relative would have for another. In other words, to be kind to someone meant to view them as kin—as family. To be loving, compassionate, inclined to help, determined to do good rather than harm.

Kinship is a good explanation of how God shows

kindness to his people: he treats them as family. In the Garden he made clothes for Adam and Eve to cover their shame (Genesis 3 v 21). In the desert he "led [the Israelites] with cords of human kindness, with ties of love" (Hosea 11 v 4). He showed kindness to Joseph in prison by making the warden sympathetic towards him (Genesis 39 v 21). He cared for Naomi and Ruth by providing work and protection for Ruth in the field of a man who would later marry her. Even as Naomi grieved for her husband and sons, she knew that "[God's] kindness has not forsaken the living or the dead!" (Ruth 2 v 20, ESV).

The perfect expression of God's kindness is Jesus. He shows us what true kindness looks and sounds like. If we want to learn to speak kindly, we need to look to him.

> *But when the kindness and love of God our Saviour appeared, he saved us, not because of righteous things we had done, but because of his mercy. (Titus 3 v 4-5)*

SOMEONE'S DAUGHTER

The woman stood behind Jesus, weeping. Her tears fell onto his feet as he reclined by the low dinner table. She bent down, ignoring the other guests, and wiped his feet dry with her hair. Then she kissed them and poured perfume on them. If this were filmed close up, it would make a moving scene.

Simon, the host of this meal in Luke 7, did not view the woman as someone worth identifying with. He saw only her unworthiness to approach his table and speak with his guests. And he despised Jesus for allowing her near him. He felt no compassion or sympathy for her. He saw himself as socially and morally superior, and had nothing kind to say at all.

But Jesus had no contempt for this woman. He knew her past. He knew why she was despised by the respectable and religious. He knew her sin, her shame and her sincere love for him—the one who could forgive it all. He was not embarrassed by her emotion, but spoke kindly to her.

Your sins are forgiven … Your faith has saved you; go in peace. (Luke 7 v 48, 50)

It is likely that this woman was a prostitute. But Luke introduces her first as a woman (Luke 7 v 37). She had lived a sinful life, but she was a human being like him— made in the image of God with inherent dignity and worth. Someone's daughter. Someone's sister. Someone's neighbour. Her sinful past did not erase her humanity. She was kin.

And that is how Jesus treated her too. A sinner in need of forgiveness, yes. But a woman he was willing to associate with and show kindness to.

Kindness means seeing the image of God in everyone, regardless of their shocking past or messy present. It means recognising our shared status as image-bearers and treating one another accordingly. When we belittle, criticise or patronise someone, our words show that we do not value them as we should. But to speak kindly—even as we disagree with a person's beliefs or actions—is to acknowledge our shared humanity and our shared need for grace.

Simon needed to understand that his position as a Pharisee did not make him more righteous than the woman kissing Jesus' feet. Both were sinners and both were equally in need of mercy and forgiveness. He could not afford to sneer at Jesus' welcome of "sinners", because he was a sinner himself. Jesus corrected Simon's wrong thinking, first with a parable and then with some direct comments about his behaviour (v 40-47—notice that his strategy is rather similar to the one used by Nathan which we saw in chapter 2). In doing so, Jesus was showing kindness to Simon—he was giving him the opportunity to repent and be forgiven.

There are times when we, too, must show kindness by setting people straight. An obvious example is in disciplining children. Children are not naturally obedient, self-controlled, generous or wise. They disobey, push boundaries (and sometimes other children!), and are often impatient and strong-willed. It is not kind to allow children to persist in behaviour that dishonours God or other people. They need to be corrected so they can learn how to live well in God's world. But in disciplining children, we mustn't forget that they are kin. They are no less important just because they are small. Parents and teachers need to be clear and consistent in their discipline, but also compassionate, patient and forgiving.

Our online interactions should also reflect our awareness that whoever is on the other end of our text, tweet, post or email shares our dignity and worth. We may want to join in an online debate or correct someone who has misrepresented our viewpoint, but kindness requires us to remember the humanity of the person behind the screen.

It asks us to view them with compassion rather than contempt. And to make every effort to be respectful and civil even as we may disagree.

CHANGE MY HEART

Who do you treat as kin? It is easy to be like Simon. To categorise people as either worthy of kindness or not. To forget our shared humanity with people who irritate or offend us. To overlook the dignity of people we feel superior to. To speak sharply to those who most need gentleness and patience. I know I am most impatient with people who don't share my viewpoints or don't behave in ways I think are right. It is easier to criticise or complain than to show compassion and care. Easier to put down than to build up.

So how do we respond kindly? How can we show kindness like Jesus does—even to those we find difficult? The apostle Paul regularly links kindness with compassion and patience.

Clothe yourselves with compassion, kindness, humility, gentleness and patience. (Colossians 3 v 12)

Be kind and compassionate to one another.
(Ephesians 4 v 32)

But the fruit of the Spirit is love, joy, peace, patience, kindness, goodness, faithfulness.
(Galatians 5 v 22, ESV)

It is unlikely that we will speak with kindness if we do

not also show these other aspects of grace. Compassion will provoke a kind response rather than a harsh or dismissive word. Patience will enable us to bear with those we don't understand or who we disagree with, so our words will do good in their lives. If we want to learn to speak with kindness, we need to pray for a compassionate heart and a patient attitude towards people who are unlike us.

This is a prayer Jesus loves to answer. He not only became like us, but also makes us like him. His Spirit transforms our hearts and minds so that we reflect his more fully. He grows his fruit in us (Galatians 5 v 22-23), and enables us to "clothe [ourselves] with compassion, kindness, humility, gentleness and patience" (Colossians 3 v 12). If you know your speech is not kind, ask him to change your heart and transform your mind. He can do it!

CONFRONTING WITH KINDNESS

But perhaps you're thinking, "Why bother? It all seems a lot of effort and I'm not sure my words make much difference, anyway." You're right—it does take effort to speak with kindness. It is especially difficult when we are sinned against. But in these situations a kind response can have a significant impact. This does not mean overlooking ungodly behaviour. But by speaking kindly we are more likely to help those who have wronged us to identify their sin and repent.

Paul reminds the church in Rome that the goal of God's kindness is repentance.

Do you presume on the riches of his kindness and forbearance and patience, not knowing that God's kindness is meant to lead you to repentance?
(Romans 2 v 4, ESV)

In other words, *You don't get to bask in God's kindness without letting it change you. He is kind to you so that you will turn to him, repent, and receive forgiveness.*

The right response to God's kindness is repentance. As we reflect him in his kindness, we do so in the hope that those who need to repent will turn to him and find life. In his final letter to his protégé Timothy, Paul writes:

The Lord's servant must not be quarrelsome but must be kind to everyone ... Opponents must be gently instructed, in the hope that God will grant them repentance leading them to a knowledge of the truth.
(2 Timothy 2 v 24-25)

Paul wants Timothy to be kind to everyone, even his opponents. The opponents Paul has in mind here are false teachers—people who threaten the unity of the church. Like Simon, they must be confronted with their error and corrected. It would not be kind to them or to the church to let them continue in it. But this correction must be done gently. The false teachers' errors, grave as they are, are no excuse for unkind words.

Timothy must respond to error and opposition in a way that is counter-intuitive. His natural response might be outrage or anger, but he must recognise his shared humanity and need for grace, and speak with kindness and gentleness. This will be costly for him—particularly if his opponents don't respond with repentance. But his kind words may be the means of some finding life.

This is our hope, too, as we respond with kindness to people who oppose our faith in Jesus or hurt us in other ways—perhaps through criticism, mocking, or slander. Rather than retaliate with aggressive words that may provoke our opponents to further attack, we can choose to value them as fellow image-bearers who should be treated with civility and dignity—even if they don't treat us the same way. Our natural instinct may be to recipro-cate unkindness, but the Holy Spirit can equip us to bear with our opponents patiently and speak with gentleness and grace. This may not be the only thing we need to do—we may need outside help of various kinds—but it is a very important thing.

Is there someone in your life who regularly criticises or belittles you—perhaps because of your faith or maybe for some other reason? How do you tend to respond to them? What might it look like to repay insult with blessing (1 Peter 3 v 9)? What would this communicate to them—and to those who may be listening? Pause now and ask the Spirit to help you do this, and to use your kind words to bring about repentance and life.

A PATH TO LIFE

Rosaria Butterfield writes in her memoir, *The Secrets of an Unlikely Convert*, about her journey to faith in Jesus. She was a professor of English and Women's Studies, a committed lesbian and an LGBTQ activist when she met pastor Ken Smith and his wife, Floy. After publishing a critique of an evangelical Christian group in her local newspaper, Rosaria received plenty of responses—from people who agreed with her and from those who strongly disagreed. One letter stood out.

Ken Smith had written a two-page response to her article that Rosaria describes as a "kind and inquiring letter … the kindest letter of opposition that I had ever received" (p 8-9). Ken didn't attack her, but encouraged her to explore and question her beliefs. And he invited her to call him to discuss her ideas more fully. Eventually, Rosaria called and, after their conversation, accepted his invitation to dinner at his house. Ken and Floy became Rosaria's friends, and eventually led her to faith in Christ.

Ken Smith did not agree with Rosaria's viewpoints, and he had no obligation to engage with her about them. But he chose to respond with a kindness that was so completely unexpected, she couldn't ignore it. He viewed her not simply as someone whose beliefs and lifestyle he disapproved of, but as a woman in need of the same compassion and grace that had transformed his own life. I wonder what the impact might be in my city if every follower of Jesus would choose to treat those we disagree with like this. I wonder what the impact might be on social media if all Christians would respond to alternate viewpoints with civility, humility and respect. I wonder what the impact might be in my own church family if I would commit to kind speech.

A few days ago, I sat in a meeting listening as a young woman complained about almost every aspect of her life—including some privileges and opportunities that

I know others would love to have. My response did not reflect the kindness I experience each day from my patient heavenly Father. Instead, I inwardly criticised her sense of entitlement—and congratulated myself for managing to be joyful and content in my circumstances. Today, I wonder whether I could have helped this woman by acknowledging how burdened she felt and gently pointing her to the one whose burden is light. I wonder if I could have encouraged compassion and patience in others had I modelled a kind response.

THE KINDEST WORDS

They stripped his clothing from him and beat his body. As he hung, bleeding and struggling for breath, they mocked and sneered at him, "He saved others … but he can't save himself!" (Matthew 27 v 42). They meant to insult him, but their words were true. In that moment, Jesus could not save both himself and others. He chose to sacrifice himself to save others.

Perhaps the kindest words ever spoken were these:

Father, forgive them, for they do not know what they are doing. (Luke 23 v 34)

Forgive them. To acknowledge a hurt or offense and to choose forgiveness is truly kind. These words communicate goodness, compassion, generosity and grace.

There is no greater offence than our rejection of God and his rightful rule over our lives. But Jesus gave his life so that we might be forgiven. There is no greater kindness he could have shown than to forgive his enemies. No kinder words he could have spoken on the cross than to ask the Father to forgive the sin of those who nailed him there.

As we consider the kind and forgiving words of Jesus in those last excruciating moments of his life, we should find ourselves more inclined to forgive those who hurt us. Martyn Lloyd-Jones, a 20th-century preacher, is said to have declared, "Whenever I see myself before God and realise something of what my blessed Lord has done for me at Calvary, I am ready to forgive anybody anything". If that is not your experience, take some time to reflect on Jesus' kindness in forgiving you. Then pray for his Spirit to soften your heart and enable you to be kind and compassionate, forgiving others just as God forgave you (Ephesians 4 v 32).

SWEETNESS FOR THE SOUL

What will it look like for you to cultivate kind speech in your everyday life? Is there someone who regularly gets under your skin—perhaps a family member or a work colleague? Is there someone at church you find irritating or a neighbour whose conversation you find tedious? What would it look like for you to respond with goodness, gentleness, generosity and grace? And what impact might your words have on that person?

King Solomon insists that "kind words are like honey—sweet to the soul and healthy for the body" (Proverbs 16 v 24, NLT). I want my words to have that effect on people. I want my speech to refresh, nourish and inspire growth and flourishing. I want to be known for civility and grace: a person who treats everyone with dignity and honour, even when others do not. I want to remember the kindness of Jesus in being unashamed to call me "sister" (Hebrews 2 v 11), and I want to treat others with that same kindness. Don't you?

QUESTIONS FOR REFLECTION

1. *In what ways does this chapter deepen your understanding of kindness?*

2. *What strikes you most about the way Jesus responds to the woman in Luke 7? How does it encourage you? How does it challenge you?*

3. *Who are you often tempted to be irritable or impatient with? How might viewing them as kin impact the way you speak to them?*

4. *Paul says, "Be kind and compassionate to one another". How can you use your words to show kindness and compassion to someone this week?*

A PLACE IN THE KINGDOM

SPEAKING HOPE

*Always be prepared to give an answer to everyone who
asks you to give the reason for the hope that you have.
But do this with gentleness and respect.*

1 Peter 3 v 15

"That's the most remarkable thing I've ever heard!"
Ruth was telling the group about the deep sense
of peace she had experienced throughout her cancer
diagnosis and surgery. She shared how her hope of
eternal life with Jesus relieved any fears she had about
the future, and that she could anticipate death peace-
fully and joyfully because she knew her future life with
him was certain and glorious. I watched her friend Eve
staring at her open-mouthed, astonishment written
all over her face. She'd had no idea it was possible to
live with such hope—especially in the face of suffering

and death. "I would love to have a hope like that!" she exclaimed.

I have to confess that, while I was enthusiastic about running a course for people exploring Christianity, I didn't really expect that a simple conversation could lead to such a dramatic response. It reminded me that our words really can bring genuine hope.

As Christians, we have true, certain, life-transforming, death-defying hope that changes everything about the way we live—and the way we die. Hope that, through the resurrection of Jesus Christ from the dead, we too will live for ever. This is the best news in the world, and we have the opportunity to use our words to bring this hope to people who are desperate for it—even if they don't yet realise it.

The gospel brings hope into the darkest and most desperate situations, but if you're like me, you probably struggle to speak about this hope boldly. We want our friends, neighbours and work colleagues to know the hope we have, but talking about the gospel can feel unnatural and awkward. Often, the problem is not being afraid of saying the wrong thing, but saying anything at all. We want to speak but the words get stuck somewhere between our vocal cords and our tongue.

Perhaps you've been tempted to give up on speaking about your faith—after all, there are plenty of other ways to do good with your words. But if we persevere in learning to speak hope, I think we will find that this type of speech can be the most wonderful and life-bringing of all.

AN UNLIKELY VISITOR

When Jesus came, he welcomed "sinners"—those on the outskirts of society, religious outsiders. But he also came to bring hope to "insiders"—to people whose need for salvation was less obvious. Nicodemus was one of these insiders. A respected member of the Jewish ruling council, he was an authority on morality and religion. He was wealthy and enjoyed high status in his community. He had no obvious need of Jesus; even so, he came to find out more.

> *Now there was a Pharisee, a man named Nicodemus who was a member of the Jewish ruling council. He came to Jesus at night and said, "Rabbi, we know that you are a teacher who has come from God. For no one could perform the signs you are doing if God were not with him." (John 3 v 1-2)*

We don't know why Nicodemus comes to Jesus at night. Perhaps he has simply been too busy to talk with him during the day, or maybe he wants a private meeting. The Pharisees were not typically welcoming of Jesus—he had no religious training, yet he had the audacity to challenge their authority. And he hung around with irreligious and disreputable people—not the kind of company high-ranking members of the community would be expected to keep. Maybe Nicodemus doesn't want to risk his reputation by being seen with Jesus in public.

But Jesus' miracles have convinced him that Jesus is no ordinary teacher, and he wants to know more. Perhaps Nicodemus thinks Jesus may be another prophet like John the Baptist—sent to prepare people for the promised Messiah. If that's true, maybe Jesus could tell him when to expect the coming kingdom of God and what signs to look out for. Or perhaps Nicodemus has heard people suggest that Jesus *is* the Messiah and he wants to see if that could really be true. It is clear that although Nicodemus recognises that God is *with* Jesus, he cannot see that Jesus *is* God. He doesn't yet understand who Jesus really is, and he doesn't ask the question he needs the answer to—how he can be certain of his place in God's kingdom.

But Jesus doesn't wait for Nicodemus to identify his need. He tells him clearly:

> *Very truly I tell you, no one can see the kingdom of God unless they are born again. (v 3)*

Nicodemus has witnessed some of Jesus' miracles, but he needs a miracle himself—the miracle of new birth. Without it, all his religion is worthless. He may be among the religious elite, but he is spiritually blind and cannot see his need for repentance and heart-transformation. Jesus doesn't pull any punches. He faces Nicodemus up to his problem: *You might be religious, Nicodemus, but you cannot see the kingdom of God!* Jesus has words of hope that he will speak to Nicodemus later in their conversation, but first he wants Nicodemus to see why he so desperately *needs* that hope.

Nicodemus wants to know who Jesus is, but he must first understand who he himself is. He may be moral, religious and respectable, but despite his flowing robes and prominent seat in the synagogue, he is as much outside of the kingdom of God as the social outcast down the street. And Jesus' words make no sense to him.

"How can someone be born when they are old?" Nicodemus asked. "Surely they cannot enter a second time into their mother's womb to be born!" (v 4)

Jesus has exposed Nicodemus' lack of understanding. The Pharisee has presumed that his Jewish pedigree guarantees his place in the coming kingdom and has no idea that what he really needs is Spirit-given new life (v 5-6). He has to be born again. Jesus is pulling the rug out from under Nicodemus' feet. Nicodemus cannot secure his place in the kingdom any more than he could choose what family he was born into as a baby. It all has to be a work of the Spirit.

But the rest of Jesus' words articulate the hope that Nicodemus does have.

Just as Moses lifted up the snake in the wilderness, so the Son of Man must be lifted up, that everyone who believes may have eternal life in him. (v 14-15)

Jesus will be lifted up. Nicodemus can believe in him. And if he does, Nicodemus will receive eternal life. These are the words Nicodemus needs to hear. He has a problem—but there is a hopeful solution to that problem, and Jesus offers that hope clearly. The result is transformation.

Nicodemus had come to Jesus privately, under the cover of darkness. But after Jesus was crucified, the Pharisee accompanied Joseph of Arimathea to ask Pilate for Jesus' body so they could give him a proper burial. Joseph of Arimathea had been a disciple of Jesus but had kept it secret because he feared the Jewish leaders. But at the most vulnerable moment for Jesus' followers, Joseph publicly identified with Jesus to make sure he was given a decent burial fitting—and Nicodemus was with him (John 19 v 38-39). Jesus had spoken words of hope that would change Nicodemus for ever. He had been transformed, it seems, from a spiritually blind Pharisee to a Spirit-emboldened follower.

The gospel brings real hope that changes lives for ever. It doesn't necessarily change our present circumstances, but it enables us to persevere through them with joyful anticipation of a secure future that is worth waiting for. No doubt Nicodemus experienced discomfort for publicly identifying with Jesus—all the disciples did. His reputation must have suffered. He may even have been persecuted. But he was able to face discomfort and hardship because he knew that his place in the kingdom wasn't determined by his status or reputation, but by his belief in Jesus.

That's also why my friend Ruth can be peaceful and joyful despite her cancer diagnosis. Her hope isn't dependent on clear test results or successful treatment, but on the knowledge that, one day, her body will be completely restored and will never be broken again.

This is the hope that we have the opportunity to share with those around us. If we are willing, we can play a part in bringing this kind of hope into people's lives—simply by speaking!

A LIFE FUELLED BY HOPE

Although this chapter is about sharing the gospel with our words, there is often a step that comes before that. That is what Peter anticipates when he tells us to "be prepared to give an answer to everyone who asks you to give the reason for the hope that you have" (1 Peter 3 v 15).

Peter assumes that Christians will be so distinctively different in the way they live that their neighbours will be curious about the reason why. He is writing at a time when believers in Jesus faced the threat of persecution. They would suffer—and people around them would wonder how they could patiently endure hostility and unjust treatment with hope and joy. They would ask them to explain how it was possible.

We, too, can expect this as we cope with the difficulties we face—whether that's opposition, like the persecution Peter's readers faced, or the more general struggles of life. The way we continue to live well and do good in our communities should prompt our neighbours, colleagues and unbelieving friends and family to ask how this is possible, giving us opportunities to articulate the hope that we have.

Daniel and Amy McArthur of Ashers Baking Company have modelled this well. This Christian couple from Northern Ireland endured four and a half years of court rulings and appeals because of their refusal to bake a cake promoting support for gay marriage. Throughout, they held firm to their Christian convictions and spoke with gentleness and grace—despite persistent mockery and attacks on their characters. After they won their Supreme Court case in 2018, newspaper journalist Andrew Pierce, wrote about his meeting with them:

> *They made me welcome, even though they knew I was*
> *openly gay and in a civil partnership. The cake they*
> *served me was delicious. They were a delightful couple*
> *… The next time I celebrate the anniversary of my*
> *civil partnership, I'll ask Ashers to bake the cake.*
> (*Daily Mail, 11 October 2018*)

I think this is exactly what Peter had in mind.

Similarly, when we experience grief or suffering, the way we persevere with hope should prompt others to ask why. This is what happened in the conversation between Ruth and Eve. Eve had watched Ruth face death with complete peace, and she wanted to know how this was possible. And Ruth was ready to share the reason for her hope.

Peter counsels all of us to expect this question. He assumes we are living distinctively hopeful lives. It's worth pausing here to think about how your life reflects the hope you have. When disappointments come, does the way you typically respond reflect your trust in a sovereign God who only allows what is best for you? In the face of financial insecurity, ill health or relational heartache, is your hope in the God of all comfort evident in your speech and behaviour? Are your unbelieving friends likely to see this hope in you?

And when they ask you to explain it, are you ready? You could practise now. What has Jesus done and why has that made a difference to you? Can you answer in a way that is clear and compelling? If you're not sure, ask a Christian friend if you can practise on them. Or try writing out some answers to questions you may be asked—that way you'll be prepared when the opportunities come. You don't need a clever script. And you don't need to be able to answer big theological questions. You just need to be able to share your story.

LOOKING FOR FELT NEEDS

Last Saturday I was at a conference focused on evangelism. At lunch, the women at my table were agreeing that it is fairly easy to talk about believing in God or enjoying church, but that when it comes to sharing our hope in a literal Jesus who died on a cross and was raised to life for the salvation of those who will believe in him, the words just won't come out.

I suspect the main reason many of us find it difficult stems from a fear of being rejected or of looking foolish. And we probably don't have a deep enough love for those who are spiritually dead. But perhaps we also lack faith that our words can really make a difference. Will we be able to effectively communicate the joy we experience in knowing our sins are forgiven and our future is secure? And do our friends even care? Sometimes we need hope ourselves—hope that our friends might actually *want* to hear the gospel.

Perhaps a good place to start is by thinking and praying about where they most need hope. Are they stressed about a lack of financial security? Do they suffer ill health? Are they longing for a more fulfilling relationship? Or a deeper sense of purpose or satisfaction?

In his encounter with Nicodemus, Jesus knew that Nicodemus was hoping for the kingdom of God. So he explained that he himself is the way to achieve that hope. You and I are not the answer to the hopes of the people we encounter, but Jesus is—and so we can point to him.

It might look something like this:

"It sounds as though you're searching for a deeper sense of purpose and meaning in life. I think we all feel like that at some point. Do you mind me sharing about the sense of purpose I've had since discovering Jesus?"

"I'm so sorry you've been let down—I know how painful that can feel. I guess the reality is that everyone lets us down at some point, because we're all human. That's what I find so comforting about my relationship with Jesus—it's the only one that's completely constant and secure."

"When my mum died, it felt as though the world was caving in on me. To be honest, I'm still grieving—even after all these years. But knowing that Jesus has defeated death has made all the difference. I know that one day she and I will live for ever in a perfect place. It's only this hope that keeps me going sometimes."

"I want you to know that it is possible to be free from the guilt you're experiencing. I'm not going to tell you that what you did doesn't matter. But I do want to tell you that Jesus offers forgiveness—even for our greatest mistakes. I've experienced his forgiveness myself and I'd love you to experience that too."

"I know I don't fully understand what you're going through, but Jesus does because he's lived in this broken world too. And

he longs to give you peace in this situation, and a hope for the future that is unshakeable."

Think of someone you know who seems without hope. What is their felt need? Is there a deeper, underlying longing they may not even be aware of? Ask the Holy Spirit to show you how you could gently expose that need and then point to Jesus as the answer.

All of this doesn't make talking about Jesus easy, and you may not be able to imagine yourself saying some of these things at all. When I tried out some of these conversation links on a Christian friend, she said, "You're making it sound so easy!" But I know that in a real conversation with a non-Christian friend or family member, it won't be easy at all. There is a risk of being rejected or hurt if our words don't land well. In his book *Honest Evangelism*, evangelist Rico Tice calls this the painline: it's the moment you force yourself out of comfortable, easy conversation and say something that might be met with awkwardness or hostility (p 15). It can be helpful to think about some of these links in advance, so that we feel more prepared—but even so, there's still a painline to cross. Yet as Rico underlines, if we want to see hope flower in the lives of those we're speaking to, we need to be willing to cross it.

HOW WE SPEAK

It takes courage to share our stories—especially if we are not confident of a warm response. Peter's command to be prepared to share our hope follows a call to honour Christ as Lord in our hearts. A right fear of him diminishes fear of others. But while we are not to fear people, and while we must be ready to defend our hope, Peter also calls us to kindness.

> *But do this with gentleness and respect.*
> *(1 Peter 3 v 15)*

How we speak is as important as what we speak. We must not strut our hope arrogantly or boastfully. We should not dismiss questions we are asked about it—even if they are not asked sincerely or respectfully. Rather, we should share our hope gently and with respect for our hearers.

I don't think Peter suggests this simply as a strategic way to convince sceptics that the gospel is true or that our hope is genuine—although speaking gently can diffuse anger (Proverbs 15 v 1). But gentleness and respect are the appropriate response to another person created in the image of God—another person in desperate need of the hope we have been generously given and called to share. So we will want to share our hope patiently and gently, not forcefully or with a superior attitude. Civility is more important than point-scoring or argument-winning, so pray for a gentle and humble spirit as you offer words of hope to the unbelievers God has placed you among.

OUT IN THE REAL WORLD
The easiest way to speak words of hope is by sharing stories about our own encounters with Jesus. About how he provides for our practical needs and strengthens us to persevere in difficult circumstances. How he comforts us in grief and gives us unexpected joy even in the midst of heartache.

How he calms our fears and satisfies our deepest longings. How he consistently loves and welcomes us—even when others won't. How his forgiveness of us frees us from guilt and shame. How his resurrection from death assures us that we too will rise from death and live for ever with him.

As I write, this seems so simple. So straightforward. And so compelling—who wouldn't want to meet this Jesus? But I know that when I go outside into the real world and run into my neighbour, I'll feel less sure that she really wants this hope. Less confident that my words could impact her in eternity-changing ways. If I'm honest, there are some people I struggle to believe will ever be saved—people who seem too entrenched in their lifestyles and too hostile to the gospel. Pushing through the painline of sharing Jesus with them seems pointless if they're not going to respond anyway.

But I need to trust the Spirit to use my story to give such people a glimpse of God's glory that they might not otherwise see. I need to believe that, just as he revealed himself to me through someone else's words, he can reveal himself to others through mine. That as I share with my neighbour about the hope I have in Jesus, she will think, like Eve, "I would love to have a hope like that!"

The story of Nicodemus gives me hope. The Pharisees must have seemed like hopeless cases to Jesus' disciples. They were experts in the law but did not obey it. They were more concerned with their high positions than with loving others. Jesus exposed their hypocrisy and warned about the judgment they faced because of their rejection of him. Despite their religious veneer, they were far from the kingdom of God. Yet Jesus also offers hope to everyone who wants a relationship with him—even religious hypocrites.

> *Now there was a Pharisee, a man named*
> *Nicodemus...*

It is not until the end of John's Gospel that we read about the transformation in Nicodemus. When Jesus finishes speaking with him in John 3, there is no hint that he will accept the hope Jesus offers. Of course, because Jesus is God, he knew Nicodemus would one day believe in him and receive life. We don't have this certainty when we share the hope of the gospel with our friends—but that shouldn't stop us from speaking. Our job is not to over-think how people may or may not respond, but to faith-fully pass on Jesus' promise that everyone who believes in him may have eternal life in him. What a privilege!

QUESTIONS FOR REFLECTION

1. *In what situations do you find it most difficult to speak about your hope? What do you fear?*

2. *How is hope sustaining you right now? Who do you know who needs hope in this area of life? How could you share your story with them?*

3. *Can you think of a friend or family member you have yet to "cross the painline" with? What is stopping you? How does this chapter encourage you to be more courageous?*

4. *Peter says, "Always be prepared to give an answer to everyone who asks you to give the reason for the hope that you have" (1 Peter 3 v 15). Is your life (and speech) distinctive enough to spark curiosity about your hope in Jesus? Are you ready to explain the reason for this hope? If not, take some time to think about what you would say— and pray for an opportunity to share it this week.*

7

ECHOES OF JESUS

SPEAKING PRAISE

Rejoice always, pray continually, give thanks in all circumstances; for this is God's will for you in Christ Jesus.

1 Thessalonians 5 v 16-18

The Duke of Wellington was arguably one of the greatest military leaders of 19th-century Britain. He was a brilliant strategist, most famous for defeating Napoleon at Waterloo. But he was also demanding, and rarely complimented his subordinates—something he later regretted. When he was an old man, he was asked if there was anything he would do differently if he could live his life again. After thinking for a moment, Wellington replied, "I'd give more praise".

Why is praise so much harder to give than to receive? Most of us are grateful when people affirm or encourage us, and it is easy to see how words of praise can contribute to a fruitful life. Praise motivates, inspires, and encourages perseverance. It reminds people of their value in a community, and that their contributions are appreciated. So why are we often slow to praise others? There are many reasons!

One is fear of appearing insincere. The book of Proverbs highlights the foolishness of flattery:

> *Those who flatter their neighbours are spreading nets for their feet. (Proverbs 29 v 5)*

People who praise everything they see are difficult to trust. You can never be sure whether they mean what they say—and therefore whether you really have done a good job or not. None of us wants to be that kind of person.

Another reason is worry that giving too much praise may result in pride. After all, no one wants to be responsible for someone growing a big head! Perhaps we reason that withholding affirmation may encourage more humility or a right desire to focus only on pleasing the "Audience of one".

I wonder if a more common reason for withholding praise is that when we affirm another person's attributes or achievements, we risk making ourselves look "less than" in comparison. If everyone notices how brilliant they are, it may expose our lack of ability. If we draw attention to their gentleness or patience, it might show up our weakness in these areas.

Sometimes it's just that we feel a bit awkward or embarrassed (perhaps especially if we're British!). And often, we are so focused on other things that we simply don't think about praising those around us.

You can probably think of other reasons why we might be slow to offer praise. But does it really matter? Is speaking praise such an important part of learning to say the right thing? I think the apostle Paul would say it is.

DEEP DELIGHT

It is striking that Paul begins most of his letters to the first-century churches with thanks for the people he is writing to. He is quick to affirm faith, knowledge, spiritual gifts, love for God's people, partnership in ministry, hard work and endurance. He does not seem worried that such praise might come across as insincere or result in laziness or pride. And he is not concerned that drawing attention to God's grace in the lives of others may diminish his own reputation. Paul delights in the spiritual progress of those he has been teaching and praying for—just as a father delights in the progress of his children. And as a good father encourages his children with praise, so Paul praises the individuals and churches he cares so much for.

The praise Paul offers is not superficial. It is specific, substantial and spiritual. A good model for us is found in his two letters to the church in Thessalonica. Paul, along with Silas and Timothy, writes to this fledgling church they established a few years earlier, encouraging them to continue in the faith despite the opposition they face. Their letters are not simply full of truths to believe and instructions to obey. They are also littered with praise for the Thessalonians themselves.

Much of this praise is addressed to God for his work in their lives—and we should take note of this. God is the one who is at work in the church, and all praise should go primarily to him. We must be quick to acknowledge his work in the lives of those we are seeking to encourage and give him the glory he alone deserves.

But Paul's praise also serves to encourage and affirm the Thessalonian Christians—especially in light of the persecution and difficulties they are experiencing.

> *We always thank God for all of you and continually mention you in our prayers. We remember before our God and Father your work produced by faith, your labour prompted by love, and your endurance inspired by hope in our Lord Jesus Christ.*
> *(1 Thessalonians 1 v 2-3)*

The church in Thessalonica has continued to flourish in Paul's absence—and he is thankful. He delights in knowing that these believers are putting into practice all they have been taught, and are known throughout the region for their faith in God (v 8). In their prayers, Paul and his friends express their thankfulness to God for them—and they are specific in their thanks. They thank God for the Thessalonians' work that springs from their faith. They are thankful for the love that prompts them to labour for God's kingdom. And they are thankful for their endurance that is inspired by hope in Christ's return.

Imagine how the Thessalonian believers felt as the opening paragraph of this letter was read out. They had been suffering persecution—and would continue to do so.

But Paul first affirms their endurance and hard work and then highlights the impact that it has had—the encouragement it has been to others who are also suffering. Later in the letter Paul writes:

> *Therefore, brothers and sisters, in all our distress and persecution we were encouraged about you because of your faith. For now we really live, since you are standing firm in the Lord. How can we thank God enough for you in return for all the joy we have in the presence of our God because of you?*
> *(1 Thessalonians 3 v 7-9)*

The Thessalonians' faith inspires joy in Paul and others as they also persevere in challenging circumstances. It is good for the church to know this because it will encourage them to continue, knowing that their lives are bearing fruit they cannot see. This robust, specific praise from Paul and his fellow letter-writers will have an enormous impact.

I have a Christian friend who feels very weak in her faith. She struggles with some mental-health issues that impact her life significantly, and constantly battles guilt and shame from her past. When I tell her what an encouragement her perseverance is to me and other friends, she finds it hard to believe. She considers herself weak and fragile—and the rest of us strong and sorted. So we try to share specific examples of how her perseverance in particular struggles has spurred each of us to keep going despite our own weaknesses and setbacks. We tell her that when we see and hear her singing truth (sometimes through tears), we find ourselves singing louder and with greater conviction that the Lord really is sovereign over our lives and that he really does purpose all things for our good. I hope that understanding some of the ways her perseverance benefits us will inspire her to keep going, even if things get tougher still. And I trust this kind of specific affirmation will have greater impact than a vague "Keep going, you're doing great!"

18th-century English writer, Samuel Johnson, said, "He who praises everybody praises nobody". I understand his point but I don't totally agree. I think we should be generous with our praise. But I also think that our words will only carry meaning if they are specific to the person we are speaking to. Vague sentiments do little to inspire, but affirming specific actions, behaviour or character can have a lasting impact. This means we should be on the lookout for good things to praise, as we thought about in chapter 3. Our "beauty and goodness" antennae should be up, ready to notice and celebrate the good in those God has placed in our lives.

It is far easier to criticise and complain than praise and encourage, but Paul provides a helpful model. As we read through his letters to the Thessalonians, we see there is plenty he could complain about—opposition, suffering and bad treatment (1 Thessalonians 2 v 2, 15); distress and persecution (3 v 7); lazy and disruptive people in the church (2 Thessalonians 3 v 11). Paul will offer warnings and instructions—but he begins with generous praise of the Thessalonians and assurance of his love for them. This is helpful for us to remember when we are tempted to criticise people. We should prioritise praise and thankfulness for them first, and then consider whether our complaints do really need to be expressed.

We can apply this principle to our online speech and social-media posts. Before sending a complaining email, we should pause to consider whether we could offer some encouragement first. Rather than posting a critical comment on Instagram, we could choose to share something that draws attention to the good we see in others. We don't have to join in negativity. Rather, we can use social media to praise, encourage and endorse what is good.

SPREADING PRAISE

Praise is not only something we do to someone's face—we can also praise one person in the presence of another. As we've seen, Paul gives thanks to God for his work in the Thessalonian believers' lives, but he also holds them up as a model for other believers. His second letter begins:

> *We ought always to thank God for you, brothers and sisters, and rightly so, because your faith is growing more and more, and the love all of you have for one another is increasing. Therefore, among God's churches we boast about your perseverance and faith in all the persecutions and trials you are enduring.*
> *(2 Thessalonians 1 v 3-4)*

The Thessalonians' perseverance and faith is cause for boasting to other churches—not to provoke envy or rivalry, but so that other believers who suffer may be inspired by their example. Paul uses these young believers who have endured so much as a shining example to those who need extra encouragement to stand firm in the face of opposition.

This is what we can hope to achieve with our words, too. As we draw attention to brothers and sisters who are growing in godliness, serving faithfully, persevering in trials and declaring God's glory with their lives, our intent is not to make others feel jealous or inferior. Rather, we want to motivate them and build their faith in God.

Praising people for God's work in their lives can have a positive impact on us too. When we are tempted to criticise or complain about someone, or when we feel ourselves becoming frustrated or angry, stopping to consider what is good and praiseworthy about them can change our perspective and our attitude. Even if we don't verbalise what we are thinking, choosing to focus on what is positive may keep us from losing our temper, speaking unkindly or sinning in some other way.

ECHOES OF CHRIST

As we celebrate what God is doing in the lives of our friends and church family members, we also want to be clear that it is *his* work. The point of praise is not to boost egos! We should encourage our friends by expressing our joy at what God is doing in their lives—and also let them know that we are praying for him to continue his work and be more glorified in them. This is what Paul does for the Thessalonians.

With this in mind, we constantly pray for you, that our God may make you worthy of his calling, and

that by his power he may bring to fruition your every desire for goodness and your every deed prompted by faith. We pray this so that the name of our Lord Jesus may be glorified in you, and you in him, according to the grace of our God and the Lord Jesus Christ.
(2 Thessalonians 1 v 11-12)

I don't know about you, but I would love to know that people in my church family were praying such faith-fuelling, fruit-producing, Christ-exalting prayers for me. And I feel challenged by Paul's example to pray like this for them too.

As we praise the good we see in others, we testify to God's glory and grace—and this is true even when we are praising those who are not believers. In his excellent book *Practicing Affirmation*, Sam Crabtree writes, "If anything is to be commended in others, it is because in some measure they echo—even if faintly—the character of the One most worthy of praise, the One from whom all blessings and qualities flow" (p 30).

Christians and non-Christians alike can reflect attributes of God's goodness and grace. Both can "echo" his character. And so we should be quick to point out these echoes and attribute praise to him.

Perhaps this is a new idea to you. But stop for a moment and think about some of the attributes of God you have seen echoed—in however small a way—in the lives of people you have encountered this week. Has someone shown generosity or kindness to you? Has someone been patient with your weaknesses or forgiving of your failures? Has an act of compassion caught your attention? These are all reflections of God's glory in his image-bearers. Thank him for showing himself to you in these ways—and then, if you are able, thank the person he has revealed himself through.

JOINING THE CHORUS

I put this chapter last partly because it seems to me that praise is a way of putting into practice what we have seen in all the other chapters. It's a wiser response than anger or criticism; it matters if it is true; it is a way of celebrating beauty; it can bring comfort; it is a kindness; and it points to our hope of complete transformation. Praising people is a wonderful way to both glorify God and encourage others.

But the very best way to do those things—the very best way to "say the right thing"—is to praise God himself. In chapter 3, we thought about cultivating beautiful speech that is inspired by the goodness of God we experience in our everyday lives. We saw that by choosing to think and speak about the things in our world that are excellent and praiseworthy, our hearts will be drawn towards the one who is most excellent and praiseworthy—and we will not be able to keep silent!

C.S. Lewis writes in his book *Reflections on the Psalms* that "we delight to praise what we enjoy because the praise not merely expresses but completes the enjoyment" (p 96). It is not enough to notice God's goodness and beauty—our acknowledgment of it must be expressed. Turning our reflections on God's goodness into unrestrained and exuberant praise of him is what will complete our enjoyment of him.

For many of us, however, this does not come naturally. In our busy lives, it is hard to slow down enough to praise God. Our prayers are often hurried requests or one-word expressions of frustration, fear or despair. There is nothing wrong with prayers like this—we know that the Holy Spirit interprets even our unintelligible groans into prayers that God is pleased to answer (Romans 8 v 26). But our enjoyment of God is enhanced—and completed—as we also take the time to praise him for who he is and what he is doing in our lives and in his world. What might this look like?

In his letters to the Thessalonians, Paul's praise of God is focused on the power of his word (1 Thessalonians 1 v 5; 2 v 13), his transforming work in the believers' lives (1 Thessalonians 3 v 7-9; 2 Thessalonians 2 v 13), and his unchanging character (1 Thessalonians 5 v 23-24; 2 Thessalonians 1 v 6; 3 v 3). Likewise, in his letters to other churches Paul again praises God for his word (e.g. 2 Timothy 3 v 16), his works (e.g. Colossians 2 v 13-15) and his character (e.g. Romans 11 v 33-36).

This is a pattern we find in the Psalms too. The psalmists praise God for his character (Psalm 9 v 7-10; 18 v 1-2; 89 v 1-2, 5-8; 106 v 1), his works (Psalm 92 v 4-5; 105 v 1-2; 150 v 2) and his word (Psalm 19 v 7-8; 33 v 4, 6, 9; 119 v 89, 105, 111). Word, works, character: these are good places for us to start.

What aspect of God's character could you thank him for today? Where have you seen his transforming work in someone's life? What have you read in his word recently that has encouraged, comforted or challenged you in some way? Pause now and praise him for these things.

Then take some time to think about how you can make praise a more regular part of your time speaking with God. Are there moments in your day where you could stop and praise God for his character or for his work or word? I find it helpful to pause at lunchtime to offer a prayer of praise, specifically thanking God for ways in which I've experienced his goodness or faithfulness so far that day. When I read my Bible in the mornings, I try to write out a short prayer of praise picking up on something I've read about his work in and through his people throughout history. Your rhythms and habits will be different to mine, but I encourage you to think about what might work well for you, and make a plan—if you don't plan, it will be hard to make this a habit!

Psalm 19 reminds us that creation is always declaring God's praise:

The heavens declare the glory of God;
the skies proclaim the work of his hands.
(Psalm 19 v 1)

David, who wrote this psalm, observes that creation persistently testifies to the glory of God. Without words, the skies proclaim his greatness day after day, and night after night—and the whole world hears their praise. So, as singer-songwriter Andrew Peterson says:

"Since creation is going to declare [God's great
faithfulness] either way, we may as well jump in …
and join the chorus." (Adorning the Dark, p 33)

SHOUT WITH THE STONES

Praising God is not something we must do alone. One of the joys of belonging to a church family is that each week we get to praise God together—it is one of the ways we can glorify him and encourage others at the same time.

In his book, *Spiritual Disciplines Within the Church*, Donald Whitney explains that just as a winning sports team gets more glory when a game is televised and shown to millions of viewers, so God gets more glory when his people worship him together rather than as individuals. He writes, "Public glory obviously brings more glory than does private glory. Likewise, God gets more glory when you worship him with the church than when you worship him alone." (p 77)

This is a good enough reason to prioritise corporate praise—but it is good for us too. It is life-giving, healing and transforming. Praising God together renews our perspective when we have lost sight of what is truly important in this life. It reminds us that we belong to each other, and encourages us to value and honour one another as we should. It helps us view our pain and suffering in the light of eternity, and equips us to persevere when life on this earth is hard. There are lots of things in this world that can detract and distract us from gathering regularly with God's people, but those who have glimpsed his goodness and glory will delight to join in praising him together. And since this is what we will do for eternity, we may as well get practising now!

One of my favourite moments in the Gospels is when Jesus is riding down the Mount of Olives towards Jerusalem, accompanied by a crowd of worshipping disciples. As they loudly offer their praises to God for all the miracles they have witnessed, the Pharisees tell Jesus to rebuke them. He answers:

I tell you … if they keep quiet, the stones will cry out.
(Luke 19 v 40)

One day, as Psalm 148 tells us, all creation will join together in praising God. Angels and heavenly hosts; sun, moon and shining stars; the heavens above and the oceans below; lightning, hail, snow, clouds and winds; mountains, hills and trees; wild animals and cattle; small creatures and flying birds; kings of the earth and nations; young men and women; old men and children. Let's not keep quiet, but join with all nature in declaring his praise. After all, if there's one "right thing" to say, it's this: Jesus is worthy!

QUESTIONS FOR REFLECTION

1. *What things hinder you from praising God and praising other people more? How does this chapter encourage you to prioritise praise in your daily life?*

2. *Is there someone you know who feels they are not growing in spiritual maturity as much as they'd like? What specific words of praise could you offer to encourage them and motivate them to persevere?*

3. *Where have you recently seen echoes of God's character in your friends, family, neighbours or colleagues? How could you praise them in a way that points to him?*

4. *Paul writes, "We always thank God for all of you and continually mention you in our prayers" (1 Thessalonians 1 v 2). Spend some time praising God for the people he has put in your life. Pray that he will use your words to encourage each of them according to their needs.*

ACKNOWLEDGEMENTS

I am grateful to everyone who has encouraged and prayed for me during the writing of this book.

Richard, my best friend, you love me unconditionally, support me enthusiastically, and serve me sacrificially. You give me confidence to persevere when writing (and life) is hard. I am thankful for every way you point me to Jesus.

Tiana and Jed, I'm so proud of you both and can't wait to see all the good things God has ahead for you. Love Jesus most of all and with all you've got!

Friends and family who love me and know just the right thing to say to spur me on, thank you.

Woodgreen Church family, my life is richer because of each of you.

Katy Morgan, my editor and friend. Your gentle encouragement and wise counsel are a gift to me. Thank you for your hard work on this book, and for your example of humility and grace.

The team at The Good Book Company, thank you for the privilege of serving alongside you again.

My gracious God and Saviour, your beauty and love chase after me every day of my life.

the good book
COMPANY

BIBLICAL | RELEVANT | ACCESSIBLE

At The Good Book Company, we are dedicated to helping Christians and local churches grow. We believe that God's growth process always starts with hearing clearly what he has said to us through his timeless word—the Bible.

Ever since we opened our doors in 1991, we have been striving to produce Bible-based resources that bring glory to God. We have grown to become an international provider of user-friendly resources to the Christian community, with believers of all backgrounds and denominations using our books, Bible studies, devotionals, evangelistic resources, and DVD-based courses.

We want to equip ordinary Christians to live for Christ day by day, and churches to grow in their knowledge of God, their love for one another, and the effectiveness of their outreach.

Call us for a discussion of your needs or visit one of our local websites for more information on the resources and services we provide.

Your friends at The Good Book Company

thegoodbook.com | thegoodbook.co.uk
thegoodbook.com.au | thegoodbook.co.nz
thegoodbook.co.in